The New
Manufacturing
Challenge

The New Manufacturing Challenge

Techniques for
Continuous Improvement

Kiyoshi Suzaki

THE FREE PRESS
A Division of Macmillan, Inc.
NEW YORK

Maxwell Macmillan Canada
TORONTO

Maxwell Macmillan International
NEW YORK OXFORD SINGAPORE SYDNEY

The Free Press
A Division of Macmillan, Inc.
866 Third Avenue, New York, N.Y. 10022

Maxwell Macmillan Canada, Inc.
1200 Eglinton Avenue East
Suite 200
Don Mills, Ontario M3C 3N1

Macmillan, Inc. is part of the Maxwell Communication Group of Companies.

Printed in the United States of America

printing number

8 9 10

Library of Congress Cataloging-in-Publication Data

Suzaki, Kiyoshi.
 The new manufacturing challenge.

 Bibliography: p.
 1. Manufactures—Management. 2. Industrial management. 3. Manufactures—Technological innovations. 4. Manufacturing processes. I. Title.
HD9720.5.S98 1987 658.5 86–33715
ISBN 0–02–932040–2

*To our never-ending quest
for progress*

Contents

CONTENTS

Preface

In terms of individual techniques, there is nothing outstandingly new in this book. Everything under the sky has been known to everybody. The challenge, however, is to utilize our ingenuity and listen to our common sense, and to create an environment for using them.

In this book, you will find ingenious manufacturing techniques applied in many actual cases and you will learn how they are integrated to produce powerful results. You will find how people have challenged conventional wisdom, and how different organizations have worked together in accomplishing the goals of the whole organization. You will also find how wasteful factories and offices can be in our environment, and how much they can be improved.

World competition is intensifying. Market demand is changing rapidly. As someone once commented, even if we are on the right track, we may be run over if we just sit there. As the author of this book, therefore, I would like to wish many successes to those who seriously *challenge* themselves to create a better workplace.

For those people at the shop floor, this book will give techniques and insight for continuous improvement.

For people in the office, this book will provide the opportunity to bridge the gap with the shop floor. Also, this book will provide a way to think about the application of a similar discipline in the office environment.

For top management, this book will serve to put integration of the company's operation in a better perspective, by tying people and techniques together in establishing competitive positions.

For students at school, this book will help provide advance

knowledge of the real manufacturing world . . . what it is like and what skills are required for entry into it. Since there are a lot of exhibits and easy terms used in this book, even a beginner should be able to follow the text without much difficulty.

Any revolutionary change requires a large amount of energy. I simply hope that this book will provide ways for people to meet the challenge of their new endeavors.

Critiques, questions, or suggestions about the book should be addressed to the author at 1137 El Medio Avenue, Suite 101, Pacific Palisades, California 90272.

Acknowledgments

This book reflects the contributions of many people with whom I have had long and close relationships. I am indebted to the many who have encouraged and supported me in various ways through my work as well as in completing this book.

In industry, I am most indebted to the people at Toyota Motor Corporation and their affiliated companies for my exposure to the management philosophy, concepts, and techniques incorporated in the Toyota Production System. I am also indebted to the people at Toshiba Corporation, where I spent my first ten years working as an engineer. Also, to the Boston Consulting Group where I started my consulting career.

In the academic field, I am especially thankful for the contributions of Professor Steven C. Wheelwright of Stanford University, Professor Robert Hall of Indiana University, Dr. Richard J. Schonberger of Schonberger & Associates in Seattle, Dr. W. Edwards Deming in Washington, D.C.; in West Germany, Professor Horst Wildemann of Passau University; and, in Japan, Professor Jim Nakane of Waseda University, Professor Shigeru Mizuno of Tokyo Institute of Technology, Professor Hajime Yamashina of Kyoto University, and Professor Yasuhiro Monden of Tsukuba University.

In industry, I have worked with and/or exchanged ideas with many companies in the United States, Europe, and Asia. Many of these companies have given permission to use the material in this book. While it is impossible to list all the names of the companies to which I am thankful, I would especially like to express my appreciation to the following companies and their people.

ACKNOWLEDGMENTS

From the United States: Amot Controls, Apple Computer, Auburn Gear, Bay City Containers, Blount, Inc., Borg-Warner, Cosmair, CTS Corporation, Cummins Engine, Fireplace Manufacturers, Inc., Firestone, FMC, Ford, General Electric, General Motors, Harley-Davidson, Hewlett-Packard, IBM, Motorola, Omark Industries, Pacific Scientific, Priam, Puritan-Bennett, Rockwell International, Tektronix, TRW, Westvaco, Whittaker, Worldmark, Xerox.

From Europe: Daimler Benz, F. L. Smith, Haviland, Land Rover, L'Oréal, Neuhaus, Plastic Omnium, Saab, Siemens.

From Japan: Aishin, Canon, Daihatsu, Fujitsu, Hitachi, Hitachi Kenki, Honda, Iseki, Isuzu, Kanto Auto Works, Komatsu, Kubota, Matsushita, Mazda, Mitsubishi, NEC, Nippondenso, Ricoh, Sanyo, Sharp, Sony, Suzuki, Tokai Rika, Tokyo Electric Co., Tokyo-Juki, Toshiba, Toyota, Yamazaki Machinery, Yanmar.

Through my work I have made acquaintance with many people. Unfortunately, I cannot possibly list all their names here. However, a few of those whom I cannot forget are, for example, an operator who made a wonderful presentation to top management, a supervisor who could not sleep well the night before a new line layout startup, a quality assurance manager who told me that his job is to eliminate his job by education and delegation.

Also, there were managers and union negotiation team members with whom I spent time both at the negotiation table and at the dinner table, a company president whom I took on a Japanese factory tour and who later shared with me his pleasure about a big new contract award that was closely tied to the much-improved factory operations, and operators in a company where the average number of suggestions per employee has constantly increased from zero to the current level of more than three suggestions per employee per month, including one operator who made fifty-two suggestions in one month.

Many of the people mentioned above are in the United States. Outside of the United States, however, there are also many people to whom I am indebted. From Japan, there are many who have influenced me to open my eyes by their dedicated efforts toward creating new production systems. Especially influential have been Mr. Taiichi Ohno of Toyota, who is also known as the father of just-in-time production, Mr. Tetsuo Kondo of Kibun, and Mr. Akitsugu Moriya of Kanto Auto Works. Mr. Majima and Mr. Nurishi of Factory Management and Mr. Hirano of Soft Plaza Ltd. have been helpful in publishing more than a dozen of my articles in *Factory*

Management magazine in Japan as well as in contributing many ideas for this book. Mr. Oguro of Diamond Publishing Company has also been supportive in sharing my ideas through publishing my book in Japan.

From France, Mr. Jean Bounine and Mr. Francois Dalle from L'Oréal have been helpful to me in sharing my belief in their organization and others, as well as in publishing a book co-authored by Mr. Bounine and myself in French. Furthermore, Mr. Patrice Blank of Liaison Sociales has been supportive in introducing me to French government officials as well as industry executives.

From other European countries, as well as from Asia, I have been engaged by many people in various industries and in various institutions. I can only appreciate our exchanges, which were most meaningful to me in developing a broader and clearer picture of people's needs and their characteristic problems.

From Arthur Young & Company, I am thankful to Karen Hall and Kathy Gibbons for their efforts on my manuscript. Also, my colleagues, especially Deward Watts and Lee Sage, have been a help in supporting my work. I also appreciate John Schornack and Tom Gunn for giving unvoiced support to me.

From The Free Press, I am especially thankful to Bob Wallace, Celia Knight, and support staffs for their patience in working with my manuscript. I will not forget that this book has created a "new manufacturing challenge" for their publishing operations.

For personal as well as professional support, I am thankful to Barbara Walk, Fred Newman, Jim Connor, Bill Harris, and John Hornsby; without them I am doubtful if this book would have ever been completed. Also, I am grateful to all readers and contributors to my periodical, *The Eucalyptus News,* through which many precious experiences and visions of a new manufacturing world have been shared.

Last but not least, I am thankful to my parents, mentors, friends, and colleagues, who have guided me to this point today.

I certainly hope that the voices and energies of the many people I have encountered will somehow be conveyed through this book. The best acknowledgment to them, I believe, is for readers to internalize and apply the ideas, techniques, and concepts that are presented.

Introduction

During the past several years, I have helped a number of Fortune 500 companies and small manufacturers implement just-in-time production, total quality control, and total productive maintenance concepts in their factories. One company, for example—a worldwide leader in transportation equipment—told me its share of the market was eroding significantly because of competition from Japan, Europe, and other parts of the world.

On my first visit, I walked around the shop floor where thousands of people were working. It soon became obvious to me that there were about twice the people required, twice the required space, and far too much inventory and scrap.

Why was such a situation unnoticed or left alone for such a long time? There were robots, numerical control (NC) machinery, new equipment, computer terminals, and an automated warehouse on the shop floor. But somehow, things were not coordinated well. In fact, I noticed that the use of several pieces of equipment was clearly a waste of money.

Most of the engineers were busy planning new equipment purchases rather than involving themselves in fundamental improvement activities. The union people were skeptical of management, maintenance people were fighting fires and were slow to respond to requests from production people. There were many inspectors, but not much statistical process control was practiced.

I have seen many factories like this in the United States and other parts of the world. At the same time, I have met many people who were concerned about intensified competition and looking for ways

to regain their firms' competitive strength. There are many successes happening in various companies. Excitement is being generated on the shop floor. The question is how to accelerate the pace of necessary changes.

Among the industries discussed in this book are automotive, electric and electronic, telecommunication, computer and peripherals, aerospace and defense, household, oil exploration, sports, textile, cosmetics and toiletries, tire, paper, laser, nuclear, medical, and construction equipment. Company profiles vary from less than $10 million to more than $10 billion in sales volume, from high growth to mature businesses, and from less than a hundred to thousands of employees per factory. Some are unionized; others are not.

Many of the techniques described in this book may appear common sense to many people—after the fact. Some of these techniques have been overlooked by management because of their very simplicity and their orientation to the shop floor. Accordingly, success will not be achieved by directing people from the office. But for those who have patience and are challenged to practice new ideas and involve people in the process in the workplace, there is substantial benefit to be gained from this book.

Even though the challenge may at times be painful, I hope readers will create their own vision of the future, and to apply the ideas, techniques, and concepts presented in this book to their improvement endeavors.

The history of mankind has taught us that if we can imagine it, we can make it. A number of companies are meeting this challenge, as the following examples indicate.

Examples

1. A telecommunication equipment manufacturer on the West Coast has been involved in just-in-time (see page 5 for definition) as an approach to challenge for survival from intensified competition. The following illustrations indicate how improvement can be accomplished. (See Exhibit 1.)

2. An automotive parts manufacturer in the Midwest has rearranged machines to make the materials flow smoother. The results include: floor space savings of 37 percent, in-process inventory reduction of 99 percent, labor productivity increase of 54 percent, and scrap reduction of 74 percent. The cost incurred to rearrange the

Exhibit 1. Just-in-Time Approach to Manufacturing Improvements

Before just-in-time was incorporated, product manufacturing took seven to ten weeks. Today, the same product is completed in less than one week.

A product assembly area that used to cover 2000 square feet has been reduced to 400 square feet while maintaining a high-volume output.

Before just-in-time, first-pass acceptance rate was between 62 and 82 percent. Using just-in-time, first-pass acceptance rate has increased to 99 percent.

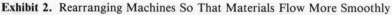

Exhibit 2. Rearranging Machines So That Materials Flow More Smoothly

machines was about $5000. The annualized cost savings was above $150,000.

An operator mentioned to me with excitement, "Things are much easier now. I can produce more with much less effort. I am happy that I am not producing defects anymore."

3. A Canadian tire factory has been working on greater involvement of all employees over the last several years. With the people's commitment as a foundation, a simple card system was introduced in the summer of 1984. As a result of this effort, a significant reduction of inventory was achieved as shown in the exhibit below.

In terms of structure, the book introduces the basics of a practice-oriented approach for improvement of manufacturing operations and presents numerous examples. Since the process of improvement is by nature never ending, the book does not necessarily emphasize a theoretical construct at the outset. Rather, this book is written to provide ideas for readers and for them to use their own creativity.

Each technique and its application may involve only certain groups of people, but a broader view of manufacturing and its related activities will be gained by reading the entire book. Since the problems in organizations are often found at the organizational

Exhibit 3. Reduction of Inventory Level

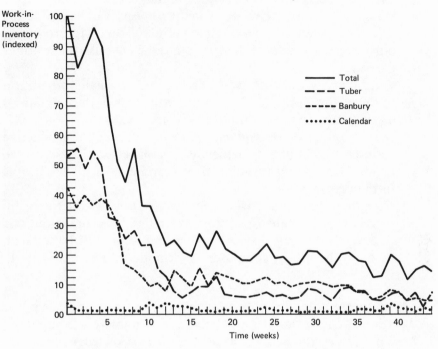

boundaries, understanding the linkages among different groups within the organization becomes critical for streamlining operations.

Viewing operations as a whole is important for another reason: In order to make progress, we must be able to observe our work without preconceived notions. Simply looking at the problem from a personal point of view is not enough. While it is our natural tendency to protect our own turf and try to prove that someone else is responsible for the problem, we should open our minds and face the reality. Instead of thinking that our situations are different or that problems are not our responsibility, I would like each of us to challenge the present state of affairs, to take a look at the problem from different perspectives, and to develop necessary skills and visions for our progress.

Application of techniques is a first step, integration of different techniques is a second step, but "internalizing" the process of improvement by people will undoubtedly enhance the progress much further.

Readers should note the meanings of some terms that are used frequently in the book:

- *Just-in-Time (JIT) Production:* a management philosophy aimed at eliminating waste from every aspect of manufacturing and its related activities. The term JIT refers to producing only what is needed, when it is needed, in just the amount needed.
- *Total Quality Control (TQC):* a concept of quality operation of the business with all the people in all areas of the company's organization involved to meet customer needs.
- *Total Productive Maintenance (TPM):* a concept of productive maintenance aimed at achieving overall effectiveness of the production system through the involvement of all the people in the organization.
- *Computer Integrated Manufacturing (CIM):* a concept to integrate the company operations from design, production, and distribution to after-sales service and support in the field, through the use of computers and modern information technologies.

Also, please note that only a few names of organizations appear in this book. While examples are derived from numerous companies, I chose not to cite their names except in the acknowledgments. This is because: (1) readers will gain more by focusing their attention on the generic nature of the improvement process rather than on the specific names of organizations, and (2) some companies wanted to disguise their names because of the very competitive nature of their business. A point to remember is that these improvements are taking place in many organizations in various industries around the world.

Chapter 1

Eliminating Waste

Unfortunately there is too much waste in our work environment. While we talk constantly about the difficulties in making money, we tend to ignore the waste that surrounds us and to overlook opportunities for improvement.

We tend to look at time as something that *adds* value. Job experience, for example, is considered a function of time based on accumulated experiences or hours spent in producing goods. Instead, we should view time as something that *erodes* value when it is misspent. We should take specific actions to accelerate the improvement of operations and thereby run our workplaces more efficiently—so that we can move forward.

SCENES IN THE FACTORY

Before talking about what we can or should do to improve our workplaces, let us first get a few comments from the people in the factory:

> *Shop foreman:* "Most of our people are working very hard. We are doing everything possible to improve our practice here. It just takes time for us to get to where we want to be."
>
> *Plant manager:* "We have many things going on in our factory. We are doing SPC [statistical process control] training and quality circle activities. We have implemented a suggestion program. We have MRP [material requirements planning]. We have even introduced robotics and an automated warehouse. But somehow, I have a feeling that things are not going well. For example, the number of sug-

7

gestions is low, machines are still breaking down, quality level is not as high as I want to see it, sudden schedule changes are still common, and so on. Because of these things, I spend too much time chasing fires and attending daily meetings."

Chief executive officer: "I don't know what's going wrong. I have attended seminars and conferences; I have looked around and hired consultants for help. But what I have accumulated so far are lots of documents, papers, fragments of thoughts, and so on. Somehow I haven't been able to integrate them into a plan of action yet."

These are comments I hear quite often. People are concerned about day-to-day problems, fires in the factory, and the like. They are attending seminars and reading about new management techniques. But they are missing something they need to know, and they feel confused. Perhaps there is even feeling of resignation (or satisfaction) that people have done their best and cannot do better.

While developing an integrated understanding and setting priorities are important processes in our work, a fundamental question is whether we have spent enough time finding out what's really happening on the factory floor. So, let us spend some time here to review some typical operations found in the factory.

In one area, we see an operator carrying a heavy workpiece by hand. In another area, we see people working frantically to stay on schedule after finding that an entire batch produced a few hours earlier was out of tolerance. We also see people watching a machine run, sorting good parts and bad parts, waiting for the delivery of material, stacking up inventory, and fixing machine breakdowns. When we check the way people are producing, we find they may be working just because materials are there to work on, rather than following certain prescribed procedures or disciplines (see Exhibit 1.1).

We need to ask ourselves "How many of these activities are absolutely necessary for our production activities?" and "How many of these activities are adding value to the product—rather than cost?" Or we might ask ourselves, "how many of these activities are related to things the customer sees and cares about?"

WASTE

Fujio Cho of Toyota defines *waste* as "anything other than the minimum amount of equipment, materials, parts, space, and worker's time, which are absolutely essential to add value to the product."

Exhibit 1.1. Scenes in the Factory

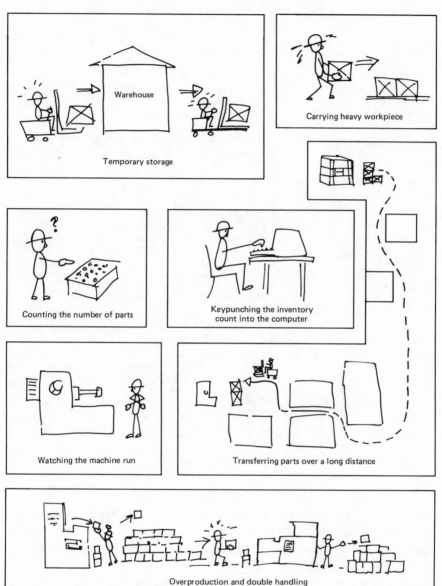

Warehouse

Temporary storage

Carrying heavy workpiece

Counting the number of parts

Keypunching the inventory
count into the computer

Watching the machine run

Transferring parts over a long distance

Overproduction and double handling

Exhibit 1.1. (*continued*)

As early as the 1920s Henry Ford was concerned with the problem of waste. He discussed it specifically in his book *Today and Tomorrow,* which Toyota people diligently studied later. To put it in simple terms, "If it doesn't add value, it's waste."

When we review the time people spend in the factory, for example, we often find that more than 95 percent of an operator's time is not being utilized to add value to the product. Rather, it is adding cost to the product. When we measure the material being processed in the factory, we may also find that, during more than 95 percent of the time, that material is in storage, waiting to be transferred, processed, or inspected. Similarly, a machine may be producing un-

necessary or defective products, or it may be broken down or require maintenance. In either case, it is obviously not being used to add value to the product. Exhibit 1.2 is a graphic representation of the problem.

People may say, "We know all of that." But the questions we should ask ourselves are, "Then what are we actually doing to reduce this waste?" "How much of our time is spent on eliminating this waste?" "Do we really know how much of this waste can be eliminated?" "Do we really know how much dollar savings can be achieved through such efforts?"

Unfortunately, most of us cannot answer these questions. One thing we should remember is that a lot of our work requires immediate action. The urgency of such matters can keep us from analyzing and planning our work. We may feel we have accomplished

Exhibit 1.2 How Man, Machine, and Material Spend Time in the Factory

How People Spend Time in Typical Factory

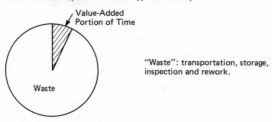

Value-Added
Portion of Time

Waste

"Waste": waiting for materials, watching machine running, producing defects, looking for tools, fixing machine breakdown, producing unnecessary items, etc.

How Materials Spend Time in Typical Factory

Value-Added
Portion of Time

Waste

"Waste": transportation, storage, inspection and rework.

How Machines Are Utilized in Typical Factory

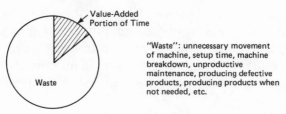

Value-Added
Portion of Time

Waste

"Waste": unnecessary movement of machine, setup time, machine breakdown, unproductive maintenance, producing defective products, producing products when not needed, etc.

more when we spend time on urgent work and exhaust ourselves. But is it really a productive way of using our time? The following portion of this chapter is devoted to answering these questions.

Seven Wastes

What we are talking about here is the need to introduce production improvement practices where the action is taking place, that is, on the shop floor. By diligently practicing problem solving with as many people as possible, many of our current problems will disappear.

While each person's ideas will be used to facilitate the improvement of factory operations, the most powerful results can be obtained by implementing improvement activities in the most integrative fashion so that each island of improvement can be tied together with the others. Also, we want to develop certain approaches to facilitate these improvements so that the improvement process becomes effective. In order to achieve such goals, we need to understand more about waste in the factory.

While products made in each factory may be different, the typical wastes found in factories are very similar. After years of improvement activities, Toyota identified the following seven types of waste as the most prominent ones.

Exhibit 1.3. The Seven Wastes

1. Waste from overproduction
2. Waste of waiting time
3. Transportation waste
4. Processing waste
5. Inventory waste
6. Waste of motion
7. Waste from product defects

Waste from overproduction. Toyota concluded that overproduction is one of the worst wastes commonly found in factories. This waste is created by producing goods over and above the amount required by the market. When the market is in an upswing, this waste may not be prominent. However, when market demand slows, the

Exhibit 1.4. By-products of Overproduction

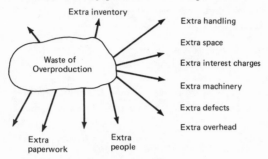

Overproduction creates more problems and
obscures the real cause of the problems.

effects of overproduction are compounded and companies often get
into trouble carrying unsold goods as extra inventory.

Overproduction waste is typically created by getting ahead of the
work. When this happens, more raw materials are consumed and
wages are paid for unneeded work, thereby creating unnecessary in-
ventory. This in turn requires additional handling of materials, ad-
ditional space to hold inventories, and additional interest paid to the
bank for money used to carry the inventories. It may also require
additional people to monitor inventories, additional paperwork, ex-
tra computers, more forklifts or warehouse space, and so on.

Furthermore, excessive inventory leads to confusion about what
needs to be done first. It also distracts people and prevents them
from focusing on immediate objectives or tasks. As a result, addi-
tional production control people are required. Since operators seem
busy and machines are occupied unnecessarily, additional equipment
may be purchased on the mistaken assumption that it is needed.

Since overproduction creates difficulties that often obscure more
fundamental problems, it is considered one of the worst wastes and
should be eliminated. In order to do so, we first need to understand
that machines and operators do not have to be fully utilized, as long
as market demands are met. (This may seem odd to many people,
but it makes sense.)

Operators at each stage of production should think of the next
process as their "customer" simply because the next process involves
working on the product produced in the previous process. We should
make sure that only the amount required by the customer is pro-
duced, at high quality, low cost, and at the time needed.

Exhibit 1.5 " The Next Process Is Your Customer"

Note: ➤ : Next process

For example, subassembly is a customer of fabrication, assembly is a customer of subassembly.

Note: This concept was originally presented by Dr. W. Edwards Deming at a top management seminar at Hakone, Japan in 1950.

Waste of waiting time. While waste from overproduction is not always easy to identify because the operators appear to be busy (even though their work does not add value to the product), waste of waiting time is usually easy to identify.

In fact, waste in the form of waiting *should* be exposed, so that corrective action can be taken. For example, instead of occupying machines to overproduce goods, operators should remain idle when the required amount of work is finished. With this practice in place, supervisors can thus better assess the capacity and control the situation more readily.

If we look around the factory, we also find operators simply watching machines run. Some may say that machines must be watched so that corrective action can be taken quickly whenever a problem arises. But is that not already too late for an operator to take action? Shouldn't there be a mechanism that automatically stops the machine and buzzes or lights up to alert an operator when an abnormal condition occurs?

Another way to look at this is that there will be no initiative to eliminate the causes of such problems because these problems are not being exposed clearly to the supervisor's eyes; instead they are often resolved by operators without a supervisor's knowledge. Even though some supervisors may prefer to ignore such problems as long as production schedules are met, should such practices be allowed?

Transportation waste. Transportation waste and double or triple handling are also commonly observed wastes in most factories. For example, incoming material may be stored in the warehouse before it is brought to the line. With such a practice, a tracking person has to be informed where to pick up the material, where to store it in the warehouse, where and when to pick it up again, and where to deliver the material down the line. He may even have to bring ma-

terials left over from the line back to the storage area if there is a lack of coordination.

Ill-planned layouts may make long-distance transportation necessary. They can also result in double or triple handling of parts that have been put away in a disorderly manner and then kept in temporary storage and switching storage locations. Often we are amazed to discover how many miles a product must travel through the factory before it is completed.

In order to eliminate this waste, improvement in layout, coordination of processes, methods of transportation, housekeeping, and workplace organization need to be considered.

Processing waste. The processing method itself may be a source of problems, resulting in unnecessary waste. For example, a certain die-casting operation may require additional labor to file and finish the surface. But a finishing operator may be quite unnecessary if the die is maintained well or if manufacturability had been considered in the product design.

Also, in manufacture of the products, certain aspects of the painting, sealing, or bolt-tightening processes may be unnecessary in meeting product requirements.

When fixtures are not well maintained or prepared, operators may have to use extra effort in processing the materials. Certain defects may be produced by these inappropriate processing procedures.

An example of improvement in a drilling operation to eliminate waste in processing is represented in Exhibit 1.6.

Exhibit 1.6. Elimination of Processing Waste in a Drilling Operation

Certain fixtures may be added or modified to facilitate operation of a machine. For example, the use of an air cylinder or chain and sprocket may help to automate the machine drilling operation. Similarly, the power of the drill machine motor may be used to eject the finished product automatically. Also, the combination of a gravity-fed chute and fixture may make automatic loading possible, thereby totally eliminating operator involvement.

Inventory waste. As discussed above in connection with waste of overproduction, excess inventory increases the cost of a product. It requires extra handling, extra space, extra interest charges, extra people, extra paperwork, and so on.

Exhibit 1.7. Large Inventories Observed at a U.S. Automotive Parts Manufacturer

Because of the problems associated with unnecessary inventory, we should consciously try to reduce inventory levels.

- Dispose of obsolete materials (housekeeping/workplace organization).
- Do not produce items not required by the subsequent process (line balance).
- Do not purchase or bring in items in large lot sizes (savings achieved through volume discounts, may be more than offset by inventory waste).
- Manufacture products in small lots (reduced setup time/more changeovers).

As we begin to reduce inventory levels, we may find more problems that need to be addressed before the inventory level can be reduced further. This is comparable to reducing the water level to expose the rocks as shown in Exhibit 1.8.

Exhibit 1.8. Inventory Covers Problems

Because of the many problems associated with inventory, we need to pay more attention to clearing out the waste associated with inventory. To emphasize this point, let's just say that excess inventory is the root of all evil.

Waste of motion. Whatever time is not spent in adding value to the product should be eliminated as much as possible. One fact we should constantly bear in mind is that "move" does not necessarily equal "work":

Exhibit 1.9. "Move" Does Not Add Value to the Product by Itself

MOVE ≠ WORK

Simply moving our hands, feet, and body does not necessarily add value to the product.

An operator may keep "busy" for three hours looking for tools all around the factory without adding even a penny of worth to the product. Instead, he has increased the cost of the product by three hours of his wages together with three hours of production lead time before delivery of the product to the customer.

We can find many other examples of this kind of waste. *Pick and place* is another example of movement that can be reduced by keeping parts or tools closer to where they are used—or even eliminated by using chutes and other fixtures.

Walking is another kind of wasteful movement, especially when one person is responsible for operating several machines. Machines should be placed so that the operator's walking time is minimized.

Waste from product defects. When defects occur at one station, operators at subsequent stations waste time waiting, thereby adding cost to the product and adding to production lead time. Furthermore, rework may be required or the defective products are scrapped. If a defect has occurred in the assembly operation, additional labor is required to disassemble the product, and additional parts are required for reassembly. Obviously, schedules must be adjusted to accommodate these changes.

Sorting out bad parts from good parts also requires additional labor. There is a waste of both the materials and the value of work already added to the parts.

An even worse case exists when customers find defects after product delivery. Not only are warranty costs and additional delivery costs incurred, but future business with the customer as well as market share may be lost.

To eliminate these problems, a system must be developed to identify the defects or the conditions that produce defects so that *anyone* present can take immediate corrective action. Without such a system, other time-saving advances are futile. Highly industrialized countries are introducing more automated machines that are capable of producing products in a short time period. However, these machines will also produce defective products at a very fast rate unless a better preventive system is developed.

SIMPLIFY, COMBINE, AND ELIMINATE

The difficulty in eliminating waste is that most of us have not directed our efforts to finding waste and eliminating it. But with more conscious effort, everybody should be able to practice this. After all, it is said that 90 percent of improvement comes from common sense. Most improvement seems so basic after the fact that people wonder why they did not think of it before. In order to acquire these skills, however, certain principles of improvement will help so that we do not have to reinvent the wheel.

Industrial engineering techniques can be basic to improving operations. But though some people may feel that improvement activity should be left to the industrial engineers because "they are paid to do it," this is not the case. We can all contribute to the improvement process. After all, who knows better about the work areas than the operators. The basic idea of improvement is simple. We want to do our work easier, faster, cheaper, better, and safer. To do so, a basic approach to improve our operations is to *simplify, combine,* and *eliminate.*

But, as with learning skills such as baseball, tennis, or swimming, this approach requires tenacity. It also requires an inquisitive mind.

So let us try out a few examples here. Looking at a number of actual examples is a way to acquire confidence in making improvements and to make developing improvements a habit.

Simplify

Case 1. In an assembly operation, an operator was using two different parts for making two different products. Because the two parts were similar, occasional mistakes resulted when the wrong part was used.

Exhibit 1.10. Color Coding Can Prevent Mistakes

19

A simple solution was developed to reduce this confusion. Each parts storage box was painted a different color to correspond to the color designated on the work order card for each job. Learning from this experience later, the product design engineer came up with the idea of using two different colors for the parts as well.

Color coding is one of the simplest methods to eliminate unnecessary confusion in daily plant operations. Corresponding bolts, tools, and dies can be painted the same color to help with quick setup operations, or lines or departments can be defined by certain colors for easy transferring of parts and materials.

Case 2. In a machining operation, an operator occasionally made careless mistakes by placing the parts in the wrong direction. This resulted in a waste of materials and shortened machine tool lives. A solution to this problem was simply to add a fixture to the machine (see Exhibit 1.11). This type of idea is called *poka-yoke* (foolproof mechanism) in Japanese. It allows an operator to concentrate on his work without paying unnecessary attention to preventing mistakes.

Other applications of this idea include the use of a template to indicate the location of certain operations, or use of a counter or interlock to check the appropriate sequence of operations.

Exhibit 1.11. Example of Poka-Yoke (Foolproof Mechanism)

Correct
(Workpiece can be loaded)

Wrong
(Workpiece cannot be loaded)

Combine

Case 3. A machining operation used two machines, each handled by a different operator. Since each machine was highly automated, the operators' time was not well utilized. They spent most of their time watching the machine operation—adding no value to the

product. By moving the machines closer together and combining the work, one operator could run both machines and still produce the same total output (see Exhibit 1.12).

Exhibit 1.12. Multiple Machine Handling

Before

After

Automatic
Load | Operation | Unload
A

Automatic
Load | Operation | Unload
B

Time

Automatic | Unload | Automatic
Load | Operation | & Load | Operation
A

W a l k | W a l k | W a l k | W a l k

Automatic | Unload
Load | Operation | & Load
B

Time

Case 4. In a setup operation, a used die was removed before a new die was installed. This approach required four steps to complete setup. A new plan, however, combined removal of the old die and insertion of a new die into one operation by the use of a specially designed cart that runs on rails. This new method eliminated three steps from the operation and reduced setup time significantly (see Exhibit 1.13).

Exhibit 1.13. Quick Die Change

Old Method

New Method

Rail

21

Case 5. To improve stamping capacity, a specially designed grabbing device (an "iron hand") was installed to take the stamped part out of the machine quickly, utilizing the upward moving force of the machine (see Exhibit 1.14). With this arrangement, the upward force, which in itself does not add value to the product, is now combined with the work of the iron hand. Since this device was designed to reach the part even before the upper die reached the highest point of its stroke, additional stamping capacity was gained.

Exhibit 1.14. Capacity Increase of a Stamping Press

Case 6. A similar idea was developed in the setup operation for an injection moulding machine. The new die is preheated using heat available from the machine. This method saves time because the die is heated before it is set on the machine and no adjustment is necessary. (Since the new die is heated, however, certain considerations are necessary for easy handling.) One solution is to reconfigure the machine structure and to prepare the new die underneath the old die, connecting them with a chain so that one movement of the crane action can do the work instead of a two-step movement (see Exhibit 1.15).

Exhibit 1.15. Quick Setup for an Injection Moulding Machine

Eliminate

Case 7. In a setup operation, adjustment typically took a large portion of the operator's time. But simple solutions can often be found to eliminate adjustment work. In Exhibit 1.16, die height was standardized so that setup was much simpler, eliminating the adjustment process. The same idea may be applied in other areas such as eliminating horizontal adjustment by providing locator pins or standardizing bolt heads.

Exhibit 1.16. Standardizing Die Height

Blocks Used to
Standardize the
Die Height

Case 8. During transfer of materials between sequential processes, unnecessary energy was wasted in double handling of the materials, trucking, and pick and place of materials on the conveyor. This waste was eliminated by synchronizing the neighboring processes and developing one-piece flow production, passing the workpiece from one operator to the next with less material handling.

In Exhibit 1.17, steps A to D illustrate the elimination of unnecessary handling and transportation. Not only do these improvements save time, but the inventory between the processes, inventory storage space, and production lead time have also been reduced significantly.

Exhibit 1.17. Eliminating Unnecessary Transportation of Materials

Exhibit 1.17. (*continued*)

Case 9. In designing a product, there may be a lack of communication between engineering and manufacturing areas. As product variety increases, the complexity of the manufacturing operation needs to be well understood and incorporated into the design phase.

One solution may be the use of standard parts for different products. The proliferation of parts is reduced, thereby eliminating the setup operation.

SUMMARY

This chapter has presented a general review of manufacturing operations from a broad perspective. We have discussed the different types of waste that are prominent in our factories and have reviewed some of the approaches for improvement. While understanding each specific technique is important, we also need to ask the following questions in the remaining portion of the book.

1. How does each of these improvements benefit the total manufacturing operation?
2. How do we integrate the islands of improvement into the total system to make the most sense?
3. How do we coordinate the implementation of these efforts?

Chapter 2

Back-to-Basics Discipline

Housekeeping and workplace organization may be considered unappealing topics to most people. People who have tried to practice these disciplines may have found them difficult to keep up. We may even try to convince ourselves that good housekeeping is an unaffordable luxury. Nevertheless, these basic disciplines must be followed by all to create a workplace everybody can be proud of.

By practicing the principle of "a place for everything, and everything in its place," a sense of standardized operations will be developed. Management by exception will be easily practiced. Furthermore, people who take pride in their workplace will be more likely to produce high quality products.

I have seen many ill-managed factories where housekeeping disciplines have not been followed at all, but all of the world-class factories I have visited are careful to follow these disciplines. For example, a West Coast company was recently awarded an exclusive right to supply a household product to a large corporation after the buyer visited the factory and found that the people in the factory were committed to housekeeping, workplace organization, quality of work, and efficiency. This was reflected in the morale on the shop floor.

Housekeeping and workplace organization should be among the first steps management takes in improving factory operations. In today's world, where management time is often devoted to number crunching and report writing, understanding the importance of these fundamental activities on the factory floor cannot be overemphasized.

HOUSEKEEPING IMPROVEMENTS

One of the easiest ways to determine a company's attitude toward improvement activities is simply to walk around the factory and review the housekeeping practices on the shop floor. If we are observant, housekeeping often tells us more about the company than any financial statement. One can judge the level of improvement activities from the way tools are stored, trash and chips from machines handled, work tables organized, inspection points indicated, factory floors swept, machines cleaned, personal items stored, and so on.

Of course, housekeeping practices reflect management's general attitude toward work. For example, a manager who pays no attention to trash scattered around the factory will influence employees in a manner very different from one who makes sure that trash is picked up whenever it is found. The point is that housekeeping ties in closely with many important aspects of management, including operators' morale, management-labor relationships, and level of improvement activities. We should understand the linkage between the level of housekeeping and the amount of defective products produced, the number of machine breakdowns, routing of material flow,

Exhibit 2.1. Clean, Organized Press Shop in a Japanese Automotive Parts Manufacturer

Exhibit 2.2. Dirty Machines and High Level of Inventory

inventory level, number of suggestions, level of absenteeism, and so on. And, if we understand this linkage well, each of us should understand better what actions are required to increase improvement activities. Housekeeping is everybody's job.

WORKPLACE ORGANIZATION

Housekeeping is tied closely to better workplace organization. What we are trying to achieve is not just clean floors and organized racks. The ultimate goal of these activities is to reduce the cost of the product. For example, in organizing dies, it does not make much sense just to pile them up. The most frequently used dies should be kept closest to the machine to simplify the transfer of dies. Workplace organization should have an economic basis.

Floors and machines should not be cleaned simply for the sake of appearance. Clean surfaces expose problems such as oil leaks and cracks so that corrective action can be taken as early as possible.

Unnecessary clutter should be avoided. For example, surplus parts that are piled in hallways can interfere with the smooth transportation of materials.

Exhibit 2.3. "A Place for Everything and Everything in Its Place"

Difficult to Handle Easy to Handle

As we examine the goods on the factory floor (e.g., parts, tools, machines, etc.), we will find that some are used often in our daily operation, while others are not used at all. Often, it is difficult to dispose of goods that are not necessary for production activities because people tend to think that they may become useful in the future. As a result, unused dies and parts inventories may be stored in the factory even though they are obsolete or for discontinued production items. These goods should be viewed as waste materials that interfere with streamlined daily production activities. They take up space and cause unnecessary recordkeeping and carrying costs.

Exhibit 2.4. Well-Organized Tool Storage Area in a Japanese Automotive Parts Manufacturer

Also, storing unnecessary goods hampers production activities by increasing transportation distances and by creating confusion in distinguishing between important and unimportant goods. Just as we take a bath or shower to wash off the dirt and sweat, our factory also needs to take a thorough cleansing periodically in order to get rid of accumulated wastes.

Examples

Use of disposal notice cards. First, identify goods that seem to be unnecessary. Then post a card to each item describing (1) what it is, (2) why it is there, (3) to which unit it belongs, and (4) when it is to be disposed of. At the end of the stated period (e.g., one to three months after posting), review the cards to see if anyone has responded with a need to keep the items. It is recommended that this approach be used plantwide, involving people from different disciplines.

Exhibit 2.5. Use of Disposal Notice for Housekeeping

```
                          Disposal Notice

          What:     Part #36GC
          Why:      Defects
          Which
          Unit:     Quality Assurance
          When to
          Be Dis-
          posed:    11/20

          Comments:
```

Monthly review. Every month, a group of people selected from different areas of responsibility should tour the plant, evaluating each zone or unit according to certain housekeeping criteria. Of course, the people working in each area are responsible for taking care of it.

The results of the review should be posted, and awards given to those who have shown good housekeeping practices. This tends to foster greater responsibility, sense of ownership, and pride. If a plantwide effort proves difficult to implement, it may be advisable to identify model areas and focus efforts there before involving other areas.

29

Exhibit 2.6. Checklist for Housekeeping and Workplace Organization

For floor, machine, jig, fixtures, instruments, dies, parts, documents, etc., the following checkpoints may be used:

Organization: Keep things close to where they belong

Orderliness: Designate location by address, line, color coding, etc.

Cleanliness: Sweep, wash, and maintain the best conditions

Safety: Safety and ease of operation are tied to respect for the individual

Discipline: Make incorrect practices visible to everyone so that correct practices are learned right away

Simplification: Dispose of unnecessary goods and simplify work environment

Storage methods.

- Provide racks for frequently used tools and an operator's work instruction sheet at the machine.

Exhibit 2.7. Key Information and Tools Available on the Spot

- Store tools near the point of use.

Exhibit 2.8. Tools Near the Point of Use

- Hang up frequently used tools for ease of access rather than spending time on pick and place.

- Identify areas for storage of inventory, hand pushcarts, etc.

Exhibit 2.10. "A Place for Everything . . . "

SUMMARY

Housekeeping and workplace organization are directly linked to achieving discipline in manufacturing. If production control, maintenance, quality assurance, or layout are not properly done, for example, then the problems will easily appear as bad housekeeping and a disorganized workplace. On the other hand, good housekeeping and workplace organization will result in better compliance to schedules, fewer machine breakdowns, lower defect rates, and prompt exposure of problem areas.

Only when these practices are coordinated can a truly first class manufacturing operation be achieved. A general attitude of cooperation should be established so that people are willing to practice good housekeeping not only in their own area, but also to help in other areas. With this as a basis, we can proceed further in our pursuit of excellence in manufacturing.

Chapter 3

Meeting Diversified Customer Needs with Quick Setup

As industry progresses, more products are made available for consumers. At the same time, more and more diversified models are appearing to suit individual tastes. Henry Ford's observation, "You can choose any color so long as it is black," no longer applies and is rarely mentioned except in industrial history classes.

Current business trends demonstrate the need to respond to market demands and to modify structures where necessary in order to remain competitive. Those who are proactive in creating the required changes to preempt the competition are often rewarded for their forward thinking. The challenge for us, then, is to develop ways to respond to a market that demands an ever increasing variety of products but one in which product life cycles are also shorter than ever before.

Obviously, we need to cut production lead time and transportation time in order to meet this challenge. We need to reduce the setup time and decrease production batch sizes. We also need to reduce inventory levels in our production and transportation systems to reduce the risk of carrying unneeded inventories.

SETUP TIME REDUCTION

Most operators, setup specialists, and supervisors do not like setup (changeover) operations. Also, machine manufacturers, tool and die makers, and product design engineers may not pay much attention to setup operations in general. Unfortunately, this remains true in spite of increasingly complex market demands.

Because of the greater variety of products available now to meet differing tastes, companies often compete with each other in offering broader product lines to satisfy specific customer needs. However, although the number of product varieties has increased, the total volume of the same product family has not necessarily increased proportionately. Therefore, the production lot size for each variety must be reduced if there is no overall increase in machine capacity.

On the other hand, if the factory had extra capacity and kept the same production lot sizes, it would accumulate additional inventory of each variety in order to meet the diversified market demand. Maintaining this additional inventory carries with it the cost of extra materials handling and interest payments to banks for investing capital on additional inventory. There is also the risk of not being able to sell the overproduced products.

In today's world competition, achieving quick setup operations is essential. By decreasing setup time, lot size and inventory level will be reduced, as well as production lead time, so that the factory operation will become flexible enough to respond to the changing market demand. Reducing the lot size also makes it easier to manage changing work priorities. These are the major reasons why setup time reduction is so important. Increased capacity is not the primary reason to reduce setup time. Instead, we need to understand the implications for the total business.

How, then, can we reduce setup time?

- The first step is to separate the work that must be done while the machine is stopped (internal setup) from work that can be done while the machine is in operation (external setup).
- The second step is to reduce internal setup by doing more work externally (e.g., preparation of dies, transfer of dies, fixtures, etc.).
- The third step is to reduce internal setup by eliminating adjustments, simplifying attachments and detachments, adding a person for additional help, etc.

- The fourth step is to reduce the total time for both internal and external work.

A well-executed setup time reduction project that involves operators, engineers, maintenance crews, and quality assurance people will boost morale, and setups of less than ten minutes can be attained in most cases.

TECHNIQUES FOR QUICK SETUP

Separating External and Internal Setup and Converting Internal Setup to External Setup

In studying time-consuming setup operations, we find the most common mistake people make is the failure to distinguish between external and internal setups. Instead, both types are mixed and treated as internal setup. Therefore, the first step is to review the total setup operation and to time each component of the operation. Then, internal and external operations can be separated.

Exhibit 3.2 shows setup improvements in a Canadian automotive company. It originally took 14 hours or more to do this rather complex setup operation which required four different skilled trade personnel. Communication among the personnel was considered a big problem.

When everybody involved in the setup was present at the machine as an experiment, however, the setup was completed in 3 hours and 45 minutes. After holding one brainstorming session and developing better communication, the people involved reduced the average setup time by almost 10 hours within one month. In order to share the progress, each day's setup time was recorded on a wall chart.

Exhibit 3.1. Separation of External and Internal Setup

Typical External Setup Tasks	Typical Internal Setup Tasks
Preparation of dies, fixtures, etc.	Attachment and detachment
Transfer of dies	Adjustment of location, height, pressure, etc.
	Test run

Exhibit 3.2. History of Setup Time Reduction in a Canadian Company

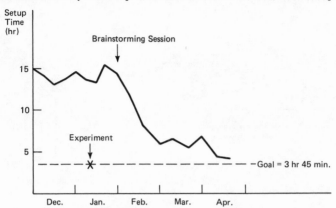

As this example suggests, significant reductions in setup time can be obtained simply by careful planning. In this case, about a 70 percent reduction of setup time was achieved without spending money on equipment.

Improving Internal Setup

Even after external and internal setups are separated, there are still usually some internal operations that can be done externally. For example, preheating the dies for die-cast machines and plastic injection moulding machines is a very effective way to convert an internal setup operation to an external setup one.

Elimination of adjustment is another key item in reducing internal setup because adjustment can take, in some cases, 40 to 50 percent of the total setup time. The key is not just to reduce adjustment, but to eliminate it by using creative thinking. Exhibit 3.3. shows two examples.

Exhibit 3.3. Two Examples of Ways to Eliminate Adjustment

Exhibit 3.4. Use of Standardized Fixtures to Eliminate Adjustment

Standardized Baseplate

Cassette-Type
Arrangement

Elimination of adjustment can also be done by using standardized fixtures. Exhibit 3.4 illustrates two examples.

In the first example, numerical control (NC) and computer-numerical control (CNC) machine setups of a West Coast defense contractor were reduced from several hours to a few minutes by using baseplates with predetermined X-Y coordinates. Similarly, a cassette-type setup is used in many Japanese companies for plastic injection moulding operations where baseplates are standardized.

Parallel operations are another way of reducing internal setup. As Exhibit 3.5 shows, people must often walk excessive distances during setup operations. This can be greatly reduced by assigning additional people to the setup. Also as opposed to the setup conducted by one operator, parallel operations tend to develop a spirit of teamwork as well.

Exhibit 3.5. Example of Parallel Operations (Top View)

Before

After

Exhibit 3.6. Parallel Work on Press Machine

Before (Total internal setup time: 57 min.)

Step No.	Operation	Internal/ External	Required Time (min.)	Performed by
1	Look for new die	I	3	Operator
2	Transfer new die	I	10	Operator
3	Remove used die	I	2	Operator
4	Attach new die	I	2	Operator
5	Transfer new material	I	10	Operator
6	Adjust	I	20	Operator
7	Transfer used die	I	10	Operator

After (Total internal setup time: 10 min.)

Step No.	Operation	Internal/ External	Required Time (min.)	Performed by
1	Look for new die	E	3	Assistant
2	Transfer new die	E	10	Assistant
5	Transfer new material	E	10	Assistant
4	Attach new die*	I	2	Assistant
6a	Adjust**	I	7	Assistant
3	Remove used die*	I	2	Operator
6b	Adjust**	I	8	Operator
7	Transfer used die	E	10	Assistant

Note: *, **: conduct operations simultaneously.

PERT (program evaluation and review technique) can be helpful in developing parallel operations. Exhibit 3.6 illustrates this point. In this case, without increasing the total man-hours required for setup, internal setup time (the time the machine remained idle) was reduced from fifty-seven mintues to ten minutes. The PERT method also helps to identify the critical path for internal setup and helps to focus efforts to make the critical path shorter.

Clamping methods can be improved to reduce attachment and detachment time. For example, the number of bolts may be reduced, the bolt head may be standardized, unnecessary threads may be cut off, and so on. Other examples are shown in Exhibit 3.7.

Exhibit 3.7. Improvements in Attachment and Detachment

Improving External Setup

Workplace organization is the key to reducing external setup work. A review of the setup operation often reveals much time wasted in looking for tools, dies, and fixtures. Designating areas by color coding shelves, assigning addresses for each storage area, etc. are basic first steps (see Exhibit 3.8). Often more time is wasted transferring dies. Frequently used dies should be stored close to the machines.

Die carts or specially designed hand pushcarts or railed carts with roller conveyors on top may be helpful and reduce the need for forklifts or cranes (see Exhibit 3.9).

Other Techniques

The use of a *setup performance chart* for monitoring setup times on the shop floor is a way to show management's concern for increased efficiency. This practice also gives operators feedback on their performance and generates an atmosphere for healthy internal competition.

The use of a video camera is often helpful in reviewing setup operations objectively. The video playback may be sped up when setup takes a long time.

Demonstrating setup operations to other people is often an effective way to motivate those who are involved in setup as well as

Exhibit 3.8. Reduction of External Setup by Workplace Organization

Exhibit 3.9. Use of Carts for Easy Die Handling

Exhibit 3.10. Setup Performance Chart

| Date | Product | | Setup Time (min.) | Comments |
	From	*To*		
5/10	A	B	20	
5/10	B	C	15	
5/11	C	D	40	die repair
5/12	D	A	10	

to recognize and share their efforts. At an automotive parts manu-
facturer, a demonstration showed how a setup that had taken more
than 3 hours could be reduced to 12 minutes. The audience of about
forty observers, including the plant manager, staff, and operators,
was extremely impressed.

The ideal way to reduce setup time is to standardize components,
parts, and raw materials. If we can avoid the proliferation of com-
ponents by increasing the usage of common components, the impact
on managing the factory operation will be significant. Close coop-
eration between the product design staff and the production people

Exhibit 3.11. Demonstration of Setup Operation

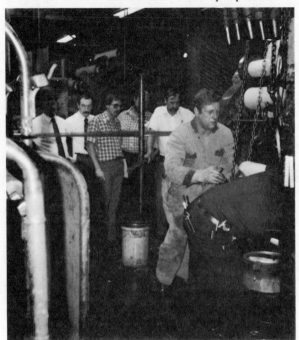

in new product development is a key to increasing the commonality of components.

Examples

Exhibit 3.12 summarizes the time study of setup operations at a small household goods manufacturer on the West Coast. As it indicates, setup operations for the 200-ton press machine took 35 minutes, 2 hours 10 minutes, 7 hours 10 minutes, and 3 hours 15 minutes respectively in this study. Long adjustment processes, a lack of die maintenance, and transportation time contributed to this long setup time.

After better housekeeping and organization practices were instituted and the need to adjust die height was eliminated, however, the setup time was reduced. In one instance, Part 34A14, setup time went from 70 down to 15 minutes in about 6 months (see Exhibit 3.13).

Exhibit 3.12. Example of Setup Time Study at Household Goods Manufacturer

Date and Time	Comments	Die
5/7		
7:00	Die change start	36OE16
7:03	Adjustment	
7:29	Inspector checking trial-run (more adjustment needed)	
7:32	Placing shims under die	
7:35	Running sufficiently	
	(Total setup time is 35 minutes)	
1:45	Finished material	
1:53	Die removed and being placed back on rack	
1:58	Next die brought to machine	36A16
2:10	Adjustment	
2:33	Rubber strips brought over to be glued onto die	
3:03	Adjustment continued	
3:20	Trial run (More adjustment needed)	
4:05	OK'd and running	
	(Total Setup time is 2 hours and 10 minutes)	
5/8	36A16 continued	36A16
5/9		
7:00	Press not in operation—waiting for next die	
7:30	Machine lubed	
8:40	No die brought to machine because NO MATERIAL available	
12:35	Die brought over also material	36B56-1
12:40	Adjustment	
1:00	Die removed—not punching holes correctly (note that 5 pcs. of material were also wasted)	
2:35	Cleaning die shoe	
3:40	34A25 was placed in operation	34A25
	(Total Setup time is 7 hours and 10 minutes)	
5/10		
7:00	Changing die shoe	
8:02	Die shoe being fastened	
8:03	Die being placed in	42A20
8:04	Adjustment	
8:30	Problem—stops on die need to be adjusted	
8:55	Welding being done on die	
10:25	OK'd and running	
	(Total time is 3 hours and 15 minutes)	

Note: Total setup times do not include time set aside for lunch or work breaks.

Exhibit 3.13. History of Setup Time Reduction at Household Goods Manufacturer

Part No. 34A14 Setup Time

Exhibit 3.14 shows a few examples of setup improvements in Japanese and U.S. factories. As the chart indicates, the two U.S. companies achieved significant improvement in less time than the Japanese.

The point here is that by understanding that there are a number of ways to improve setup times, and by practicing the basic principles and brainstorming, tremendous gains can be made without incurring large expenditures.

SUMMARY

Quick setup is a requirement for small lot production, leading to more streamlined manufacturing operations. Furthermore, it is key to developing or maintaining a company's competitiveness in today's market, where more diversified products are desired at short production lead times.

A giant Japanese consumer electric appliance manufacturer, Matsushita, for example, successfully reduced the setup time for its painting operation in the refrigerator manufacturing line. The result was an increase in the number of product varieties offered to its customers. Combined with efforts to reduce the order-taking lead time from its distributors across the nation, Matsushita achieved a 50 per-

Exhibit 3.14. Setup Time Reduction Achieved by Japanese and U.S. Companies

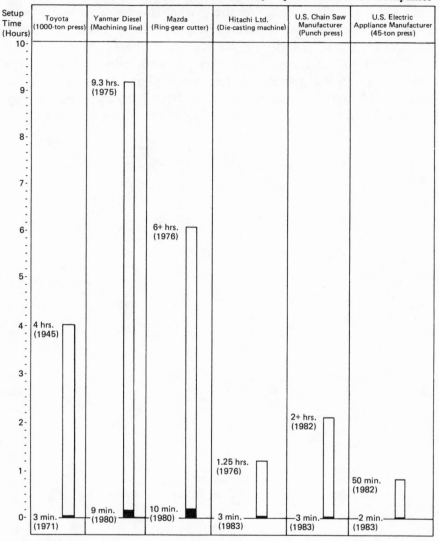

cent increase in profitability for this product as well as an increase in its market share.

As this example indicates, even in seemingly mature businesses there are ways to compete effectively if we are willing to challenge

the status quo. Other companies such as Hitachi, Toshiba, and Sanyo had a difficult time regaining the market share lost to Matsushita.

Quick setup alone, however, is not a universal panacea. As production lot sizes are reduced, we need to address other issues such as the way to handle increased transportation requirements. Here, again, it is important to link different disciplines. Unless these issues can be addressed collectively the total benefit to the company may remain small.

Chapter 4

Developing Flow on the Production Floor

In a typical factory, conveyors, forklifts, and other material handling equipment move materials between different processes. Fabrication lines and assembly lines process materials to form products. Inspection points assure the quality of products. These transfer, production, and inspection activities are fundamental to factory operations. Unfortunately, however, they are often conducted to optimize each of their own areas rather than to optimize the total production. The result is the accumulation of inventories and related problems that we touched on before.

As we can see here, problems are often caused by a lack of coordination and people's tendency to focus on their individual activities. In order to eliminate the waste associated with these problems, therefore, we need to look at the whole process of production activities.

This chapter addresses these problems by suggesting ways to develop smooth flows with better coordination of the processes throughout the factory. The first step is to scrutinize layout, and the use of machines found in our factories.

FROM PROCESS-ORIENTED LAYOUT
TO PRODUCT-ORIENTED LAYOUT

Just as serious efforts to reduce setup times have not been made until recently, the importance of factory layout has not been addressed in

spite of the significant waste often associated with badly planned layouts.

As a result, we frequently see machines placed in such a fashion that material flow is not visible at first glance. Thus, following the production processes may require physically walking across the factory floor several times.

When we question why the machines are placed where they are or why one operation is conducted a distance away from the next operation, there are typically two reasons. One is that, as factories expand, new stations are created where space is available. The other is based on the belief that similar types of machines and operations should be controlled by one supervisor in one area.

However, the waste associated with this process-oriented type of layout can be significant. In other words, the impact on a company's performance from improving the layout can be substantial in most cases, as we will see below.

Waste Associated with Process-Oriented Layout

A commonly observed machine layout is shown in Exhibit 4.1, together with the representative material flow paths. In this layout, machines of a similar function are grouped together. This type of layout is called a function-oriented layout or a process-oriented layout.

Exhibit 4.1. Material Flow in a Process-Oriented Layout

Note: ➤ : Material Flow

From Kiyoshi Suzaki, "Japanese Manufacturing Techniques: Their Importance to U.S. Manufacturers." Reprinted with permission from *Journal of Business Strategy,* Winter, 1985, Vol. 5, No. 3, Copyright © 1985, Warren, Gorham & Lamont, Inc., 210 South St., Boston, MA 02111. All rights reserved.

Although machining processes are used in this example, similar layouts, where material flow is rather irregular and long, are found in many other instances as well.

From a supervisor's point of view, the process-oriented layout seems to make sense because certain processes are under the control of one supervisor. For example, all drills are located together in the drilling department. But does it make sense from the point of view of the total production economy? To answer this question, let us examine the types of waste found in such a layout:

1. Difficult coordination and production scheduling
2. Transportation waste
3. Accumulation of in-process inventory
4. Double or triple handling of materials
5. Extremely long production lead time
6. Difficulty in identifying cause of defects
7. Flow of material and operators' work difficult to standardize
8. Difficulty in improvement due to lack of standardization.

Since consecutive processes may be at some distance from each other, communication and visibility between people from different departments are hampered and it is difficult to practice the idea that the "next process is your customer."

Naturally, people tend to focus on their own functional efficiency in this type of arrangement. Quite often, performance measures that emphasize production efficiency make the situation even worse. People are more concerned about the sheer volume they can produce every day than about producing the amount actually required by the next process. In the long run, this practice makes very little economic sense, yet it still exists in many factories.

Moving Toward a Product-Oriented Layout

Exhibit 4.2 shows an improved layout. As you can see, the material flow is much smoother than that depicted in Exhibit 4.1. Material travels according to the sequence of processes and there is less confusion about which process comes next or when and where finished material should be transferred. Processes are linked much more closely, and the distance material has to travel to complete the total production sequence is considerably shorter.

At the same time, because the lathe, paint, and other processes are decentralized, some operators may be confused about whom

Exhibit 4.2. Material Flow in a Product-Oriented Layout

Note: ➤ : Material Flow

they should report to, or about management structure in general. The roles and areas of responsibility not only of operators but of maintenance crews, inspectors, schedulers, and trucking people will need to be reconsidered.

Another concern is the potential restriction of machine capacity. Since machines are located in different areas according to the need of each product family instead of being grouped together according to function, there may be a potential capacity problem unless there is an increase in the number of machines.

This is especially true when products from several families are processed through one large, sophisticated, and expensive machine. Once such machines are purchased, they therefore, may become an obstacle to converting to a product-oriented layout.

Another additional concern about changing to a product-oriented layout is that in the traditional process-oriented layout, if machines of the same family are located in one area, operators can be easily trained and supervised, maintenance crews can become familiar with the process much more quickly, tools can be shared, and so on. When a machine malfunctions or breaks down, other machines can be substituted easily. If these machines are not in the same location, there is no such flexibility.

But if we look more carefully at these seemingly legitimate reasons to keep a process-oriented layout, we often find that a product-oriented layout can be a significant improvement, even though the conversion process may be somewhat painful.

For example, operators can be assigned to a line rather than to

a particular function. Although certain operations may seem difficult to simplify, our ability to generate ideas and our modern technology should make it possible to simplify these operations so that anyone can master them quickly. As a result, there will be much less need for operators to become specialized in a particular function.

As machines are improved to simplify their operation, operators can be trained to use more than one machine for different processes. As the operators broaden their skills, their time will be better utilized, allowing better coordination of the production processes.

Instead of using one fast, flexible, expensive machine that is shared among different product families, it is often more efficient to find or even develop cheaper machines that can be dedicated to a single line. Underutilized machine capacity in dedicated lines should be more than offset by improved labor productivity. The initial investment in additional machines may be more than compensated for by better utilization of operators' time and streamlined production operations.

Another way to handle the capacity problem is to *level* the production volume from period to period. By dedicating the line to a single product family the peak production volume can be leveled across all of the production steps from raw materials to finished products.

With such an approach toward steady production operations, bottlenecks can be easily identified and we can focus our efforts on increasing the capacity of such "bottleneck" equipment. Instead of taking machine capacity as a given, we should apply our creativity to improve capacity.

This is the process of change, and the challenge for us involved in production activities. By developing a better understanding of all areas of the production process rather than focusing on individual areas of responsibility, and by challenging the constraints rather than taking them as given, we can often make a vast improvement for all. Change does not have to be drastic; by moving step by step we will develop confidence that we can meet our challenge.

Benefits of a Product-Oriented Layout

The wastes and problems found in the process-oriented layout should be resolved by changing to a product-oriented layout. Unnecessary transportation, accumulation of in-process inventory, double or tri-

ple handling of materials, and extremely long production lead time are some of the major problems that can be improved through developing a product-oriented layout.

Exhibit 4.3 conveys these points schematically. A, B, C, and D in the exhibit correspond to four successive processes (e.g., saw, mill, grind, and plate). If we assume that each process takes one minute to complete, under the process-oriented layout it takes five minutes to complete a batch of five units at process A, and another five minutes each for processes, B, C, and D. Without adding transportation time, the total elapsed time in this case is twenty minutes for completion of the whole batch of five.

In the product-oriented layout, however, it takes four minutes to complete all four processes for the first unit, and a total of eight minutes for the whole batch of five to complete all processes. If we compare the level of in-process inventory between A and D in this case, the maximum in-process inventory is fifteen units in the process-oriented layout and three in the product-oriented layout. Similarly, storage space requirements favor the product-oriented layout.

This benefit is compounded when the number of products to be manufactured increases. In many cases, the net processing time may

Exhibit 4.3. Comparison of Process-Oriented and Product-Oriented Layouts

Note:
The distance between processes is long in the process-oriented layout, making it difficult to transfer the units one by one.

A, B, C, D : Different processes

be as small as $\frac{1}{100}$ or $\frac{1}{1000}$ of the storage time. Therefore, it makes sense to reduce the storage time in order to reduce the production lead time and to meet the customer's needs quickly. Yet, we often think that high-speed machines are preferable to slower ones. But as this case indicates, it may not make sense to pay extra for a high-speed machine if the other production processes are not well coordinated.

A change to a product-oriented layout will also substantially reduce transportation waste and double or triple handling of in-process inventories. Furthermore, quick feedback of information about defects and ease in scheduling and prioritizing work are also invaluable benefits associated with the change.

Examples

Electronic component manufacturer. An electronic component manufacturer in California took steps toward just-in-time (JIT) production in early 1985. When I visited the plant for the first time, a general manager guided me through the factory following the material flow of a major component that they produced.

It was a classic case of how inattention to the total production process can make the production flow very complicated. The flow patterns were not visible. Machines were located without regard for production sequences. Numerous tables at various locations held in-process inventories that were awaiting inspection. Parts were stored in plastic bags and transported long distances across the plant, creating waste in extra handling.

A scheduler's comment on the difficulty of keeping up with his job was quite understandable. What happened in the next couple of months is worth reporting here.

The general manager and the manufacturing manager fully understood the need to rearrange the machines to smooth the material flow. They appointed a task force consisting of a manufacturing engineer, a quality engineer, a member of the maintenance crew, a supervisor, and line operators.

Every participant on the team showed enthusiasm and excitement and contributed good ideas. At the same time operators were patient and cooperative as the team moved machines and tables trying to find the best arrangement for the new machine layout. After several brainstorming sessions, a new layout was developed and suc-

Exhibit 4.4. Product-Oriented Layout (After Rearrangement)

cessfully introduced (see Exhibit 4.4). This change reduced production lead time from three days to a mere 17 minutes.

With shortened production lead time and increased communication among operators, the defect rate was significantly lower; labor productivity improved, mainly because of less materials handling and transportation.

Even though the gains were substantial, there was still room for additional improvement. Labor productivity increases of 100 percent are not unusual when everyone cooperates. (Job security as it relates to improved labor productivity will be discussed in Chapter 14.)

In Exhibit 4.4, note that operators A and B are isolated from the rest of the group, making it difficult to coordinate jobs, especially when production volume fluctuates. Even though the current machine features may not allow them to relocate to the inside of the U-shaped line arrangement, these "isolated island" arrangements should be investigated for further improvement.

In this layout people are performing operations while seated. Typically, there is a lot of wasted movement in such an arrangement. A 10 to 15 percent productivity gain is often achieved simply by having the operators change from a sitting to a standing position.

Sheet metal fireplace manufacturer. A California sheet metal fireplace manufacturer started implementing the JIT concept in the

52

spring of 1984. The following improvement activities contributed to a very successful first year of JIT efforts:

1. Workplace organization
2. Reduced setup time
3. Involvement of people
4. Reduced production lot size
5. Leveled/mixed production
6. Layout change

Workplace organization was the first step taken along with efforts to reduce setup times for key equipment (e.g., the press machine). Banners reading "A place for everything, and everything in its place" in both English and Spanish were hung in the factory. Pictures and video tapes were shown to share the need to improve workplace organization. Dies were color coded and located close to the machines. This reduced preparation time. Also, by enforcing die maintenance and standardizing die height, setup time was reduced from about 2 hours to an average of 10 to 15 minutes.

As setup time reduction and workplace organization progressed, people became more involved and motivated. A suggestion program and a company newspaper in two languages were started to share the good things happening in the plant. As people's motivation increased, many suggestions were generated and the employee turnover rate dropped significantly.

Production lot size was also reduced during the same period. Most lot sizes were gradually reduced to about one-fifth of the previous level. Work-in-process inventory also started to go down as the lot size decreased.

Reduction of in-process inventory levels was facilitated by the introduction of leveled/mixed production scheduling where the same mix of products was produced every day for a minimum of one week. With this schedule, material flow became much smoother and operations became more predictable, resulting in fewer expedited jobs.

The plant layout was also redesigned. As Exhibit 4.5 shows, the cross flow and the long-distance transportation of materials were reduced in the new layout. Four dedicated lines were also developed, each corresponding to a product family.

The resulting significant improvements are shown in Exhibit 4.5. The company had been considering adding floor space to store inventories; instead, floor space was freed up. The operators and management now realize that there is always room for improvement.

Exhibit 4.5. Improvements at a Manufacturer of Sheet Metal Fireplaces

Plant Layout

Plant Layout (One Year Later)

Note:

▨ WIP Storage

➡ Raw Material and Purchased Parts Delivery Point

Improvement Accomplished

	June 1984	June 1985
Number of models produced	9	14
Direct labor productivity	100	128 (indexed)
Amount of scrap produced	100	40 (indexed)
Delivery period	4 weeks	1 week
Work-in-process inventory	100	48 (indexed)

Further gains for this company could result in a 100 percent increase in labor productivity as measured by output per man-hour and a 50 percent reduction in delivery time from order taking to shipping, without spending much money on equipment.

Process and Operation

As discussed above, the change toward a product-oriented layout can significantly benefit a company's operation. To understand this better, think of the factory system as composed of series of production processes and operations in a matrix form. Processes are seen from the point of view of material as it moves from one process to next; operations are seen from the viewpoint of the operators as they spend their time on each process (see Exhibit 4.6).

Exhibit 4.6. Changing Emphasis from Operations to Processes

Note:
○ Process
▽ Transfer
▽ Store
▢ Inspect

Traditionally, the efficiency of individual operations was considered more important than moving the product through the total production processes. We have been accustomed to think that someone who performs the same operation over and over will become very efficient at doing it. Yet, we often overlook the importance of advancing the steps of the production processes.

Focusing on the efficiency of individual operations worked to a degree when customers were satisfied with relatively few product varieties and the market was growing rapidly. But competition has intensified and customers now demand a variety of products with a short delivery time. Manufacturers must meet this challenge by adapting their factory operations to achieve a smoother production flow.

Flow Production

One of the most important concepts of JIT is flow production. Here, "flow" refers to the movement of material through the plant. It assumes that material will not be stagnant at any point in time from the receiving of raw material to the shipping of finished products.

Envision a river flowing smoothly through the landscape. Rapid currents, large boulders, and changes in elevation will disrupt its progress. In the same way, inefficient layouts, machine breakdowns, and many other problems can interrupt the smooth flow of production in a factory.

Exhibit 4.7. A Developed Flow Is Less Disruptive

Undeveloped Flow Developed Flow

To ensure a steady flow, some potential problems can be anticipated in advance. These may include the following:

- *Process-oriented layout.* As discussed before, parts storage time is long, in-process inventory levels are high, and the priority of work is difficult to assess.
- *Line imbalance.* If processes are not synchronized, parts will accumulate as inventory, and the coordination of work is difficult.
- *Long setup or tool-change time.* Inventory of parts may build up, or the next process may be delayed.
- *Machine breakdown.* The line will stop or there will be an accumulation of inventory.
- *Quality problems.* If defects are found, the next process will stop and inventory will accumulate.
- *Absenteeism.* If operators are absent and replacements are difficult to find, the line will stop.

In order to achieve an efficient production system, we will have to employ our ingenuity in utilizing the flow production concept throughout our factory operations. We will discuss the flow of production as it relates to machine usage in the next section, and will examine the operators' contributions in Chapter 5. Line balance, quality, and machine maintenance issues will be discussed in Chapters 6, 7, and 8, respectively.

MACHINE UTILIZATION VERSUS ON-DEMAND UTILIZATION

In just-in-time philosophy, overproduction is one of the chief obstacles to achieving efficient production activities. Because overproduction hides other problems, it is difficult to target areas for improvement. We should, therefore, aim to produce only the amount required by the customer.

When we produce the goods required by the customer (by "customer" we mean the immediate user of the product; in this case the next production process), the *machine utilization rate* should become a secondary concern. When the sales volume is high, the utilization rate should go up; when the sales volume is low, the utilization rate should go down. It is a big mistake to produce goods solely to increase machine utilization and thereby accumulate inventories.

What is important, however, is to be able to use the machine

whenever you need to produce products. We define this event as the *on-demand utilization factor*. We want to achieve a 100 percent on-demand utilization factor, rather than a 100 percent machine utilization rate. Our aim is to achieve the desired rate of production with a minimum of equipment, materials, parts, space, and operators' time. We must utilize our machines to minimize the amount of waste caused by machine breakdown, freewheeling, defects, setup, adjustment, and loss of speed.

In order to realize 100 percent on-demand utilization we need to understand the use of automated equipment. Often, low-cost automation becomes possible and the machine utilization factor becomes a secondary concern. This is discussed below.

Machine Improvement and Automation

Machines are purchased and maintained to serve specific purposes. But because manufacturers design these machines to appeal to as broad a market as possible, a machine may not match the specific needs of the user. Alternatively, machines may become too expensive to meet the versatile needs of potential users. The machine user's skill level is an important criterion in evaluating different machines as well as in adapting machine features to better fit their usage.

In the section below, we will investigate different approaches to machine improvement and automation (see Exhibit 4.8).

Exhibit 4.8. Approaches to Machine Improvement

Low-cost automation. One way to beat the competition is to use our creativity to upgrade our machine capability. If we use a particular machine the same way our competitors do, we are not differentiating our capability from theirs. The challenge is to use our creativity rather than money.

For example, operators often use drills with hand levers to control downward force. Perhaps a numerical control drill would do the

Exhibit 4.9. Low-Cost Automation—Automatic Drill Operation

work better. If we use our imagination, however, we may be able to come up with a low-cost automation idea that works just as well. Exhibit 4.9 is an example of such an idea.

An air cylinder with a rack and pinion mechanism is used to drill a hole instead of having an operator using a lever. A chain and sprocket or a wire rope and pulley may also be used to do this operation. The operator simply loads the workpiece onto the jig and pushes the palm button switch. The air cylinder moves the jig to the prescribed position underneath the drill. The machine then automatically drills a hole at the prescribed force which in turn contributes to the consistency of product quality. The operator unloads the workpiece at a later time. With this arrangement, an operator can handle more machines.

The next phase of improvement is to eject the workpiece automatically. Exhibit 4.10 shows this being done with a cam, a lever, an ejection board, and an air cylinder. The extra force of the air cylinder that is used to position the workpiece under the drill is now applied to eject the completed workpiece from the jig by the use of cam, lever, and ejection board.

With this improvement, an operator will simply load the workpiece on the jig and push the switch. The finished workpiece is then automatically ejected, and transferred by chute to the next process.

There may be room for further improvements. Such ideas as automatic loading, and automated on-off switches should also be investigated.

Exhibit 4.10. Low-Cost Automation—Automatic Ejection Mechanism

Movement of cam and lever

Exhibit 4.11 below shows an interesting case of low-cost automation found in a Japanese automobile manufacturer's stamping line where sheet metal is stamped and turned upside down before being delivered to the next process.

As the exhibit indicates, the stamped sheet metal is first pulled out by vacuum suction with iron hands (I). It is then thrown into

Exhibit 4.11. Low-Cost Automation—Stamping Line

the air and is hit by the rope which is pulled across the conveyor line (II). Inertia then causes the sheet metal to fall onto the conveyor upside down (III and IV).

The point to remember here is that these mechanisms are probably not invented by engineers. People without formal education in stress analysis, mechanical engineering, or industrial engineering often design very low-cost automated devices. Everybody can contribute his or her own creativity.

Problems associated with super machines. While low-cost automation will benefit us in improving machine capability without spending much money, the dedicated use of such inexpensive devices or equipment can also help improve flow on the production floor. In contrast to the benefit achieved by the use of low-cost automation, large versatile equipment or super machines, as such equipment may be called, often impede efficiency in the factory as a whole, even if they run very fast. As shown in Exhibit 4.12, such equipment tends to be used for several different products in order to recover capital outlays, thereby making the development of a smooth steady flow of material difficult. Obviously, we must pay special attention to this point when we select machines to meet our special requirements.

Exhibit 4.12. Large Versatile Equipment vs. Small Dedicated Equipment

Dedicated Flow Arrangement with Small Dedicated Equipment

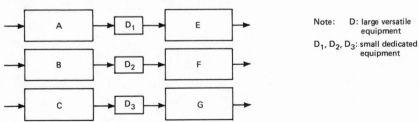

Note: D: large versatile equipment

D_1, D_2, D_3: small dedicated equipment

If we look only at a machine's capability, the use of large, versatile, super machines may be viewed as an improvement. The total impact on production, however, may be quite different. Inventory will accumulate in front of and behind the machine, requiring excess storage space. Scheduling will be hampered because of long production lead time and there will be waste in transportation. Quality problems may arise as well.

Autonomous control (Jidoka). Autonomous control means adding "intelligent" features to machines to start or stop operations as needed and emit signals for operators when necessary. This is also called autonomation (Jidoka in Japanese) and will be discussed further in Chapter 7.

As with low-cost automation, autonomous control features can often be added to machines to extend their capabilities at very low cost.

SUMMARY

The functional or process-oriented layout in which operators focus only on their own production efficiency is one of the major obstacles to developing a smooth production flow in the factory. This and other problems can be resolved by changing to a product-oriented layout. Machine improvement, automation, and machine selection also play important roles in tying each operation to the total production system.

While other problems such as line imbalance, machine breakdowns, quality considerations, and absenteeism may also impede efficiency, we must create a vision of the ideal production flow throughout the factory in order to tie the different disciplines together effectively. Without a vision of the future, there will be a limit to our endeavors.

Chapter 5

Expanding Skills for Increased Flexibility

Quality problems, machine breakdowns, and frequent schedule changes will disrupt our efforts to develop a smooth material flow on the production floor. Furthermore, rigid job descriptions restricting areas of responsibility—the Taylorist approach—also hamper the coordination of the total production system.

To address these problems, we will first concentrate in this chapter on developing manufacturing flexibility by expanding operators' skills and fully utilizing their collective skills and experience in contrast to the traditional Taylorist approach.

MULTIPROCESS HANDLING

As we saw in Chapter 4, the factory layout must be changed from a process-oriented to a product-oriented layout. Instead of locating similar processes together, different processes will be linked according to the sequence of production. In order to eliminate waste, as discussed earlier, each operator must develop *multifunctional skills* to do *multiprocess handling*.

Multiprocess handling operators in the press or machining processes may not be enough. Ideally, we want to have operators doing shearing, pressing, and braking operations, or welding, assembling, and inspecting operations.

Exhibit 5.1. Multiprocess Handling

With multiskilled operators, the production system will be much more responsive to changing market demand. We should be able to increase or decrease the number of operators on a given line with ease as the volume of business fluctuates. (See Chapter 14 for effective reallocation of people.)

Similarly, the layout should be flexible so that it can be modified quickly as business conditions change. Improvement of machines, fixtures, and equipment is also important in enabling operators to master different operations with ease. A target for management and staff might be to modify machines and fixtures so that even inexperienced operators can master certain operations within, say, three days. In order to meet this target, *foolproof mechanisms* (poka-yoke—see Chapter 7) should be developed so that operators will know immediately if they have done something incorrectly.

Furthermore, work procedures should be standardized and checklists should be prepared to familiarize operators with the work. These lists should be posted at work sites and updated regularly so that management, staff, and operators can visually compare the actual operation to the standard way and perhaps even think of new ways for improvement.

These are general guidelines and directions. Depending on work content, or work environment, and people's skill levels, some of these may be difficult to implement immediately. For example, arc welding, painting, and certain inspection work require special skills. Complete cooperation of the operators will be necessary in order to expand the scope of their work. In some cases, inflexible labor contracts may be a large obstacle in developing multiprocess handling operators.

Nonetheless, we should understand that a company's competitiveness in today's business world can depend on how each of us challenges the status quo and contributes to the organization by eliminating waste. As equipment improves and technology makes operations easier, we cannot be tied to traditional contracts or constraints. We should always be moving forward.

SKILL DEVELOPMENT AND JOB ROTATION

In order to expand the skills of each operator, additional training and job rotation are recommended. To convey the benefits of and the need for multiprocess handling to the operators, management and staff may want to consider rotating work assignments themselves.

Some people may consider job rotation for management and staff impractical, especially when a certain level of experience and special knowledge are viewed as necessary to conducting a particular job. But if we review the reasons for developing multifunctional operators, we will find that they apply equally to the development of rotating management or staff jobs. We need to develop our capability for better coordination. We must simplify our jobs as well as those of the operators so the organization as a whole can move forward.

Examples

Job rotation of foremen. In the factory of a household goods manufacturer on the West Coast, the foremen of the assembly line and the fabrication line argued constantly over parts shortages. Upon my recommendation, they exchanged jobs for two weeks. The change allowed each foreman to deepen his understanding of the other's role, and resulted in a much improved atmosphere with better communication and fewer parts shortages. Can we think of similar ways for improving communication between manufacturing people and product design people, and manufacturers and suppliers?

Job rotation of operators. At a defense contractor on the West Coast, job rotation and skill development programs were recently instituted. As each operator masters a new skill, the accomplishment is listed next to his or her name on a skill development chart posted on the factory floor. (See Exhibit 5.2.)

At the start of the program, each operator talked with his or her supervisor to coordinate a schedule of skill development which, in turn, was tied to compensation. Initially, concern about operators' reactions made some managers uneasy about displaying the chart on the shop floor. After sharing their reasons for initiating the program with the operators, however, there were no grievances. On the con-

Exhibit 5.2. An Approach to Providing Feedback in Response to Expanding Skills

Skill Development Chart						
Process No. / Operator Name	**1**	**2**	**3**	**4**	**5**	**Comment**
A	O_{78}	O_{77}	O_{68}	O_{68}		
B	O_{81}	O_{71}	O_{76}	O_{77}	O_{69}	
C			O_{84}	O_{84}	O_{84}	Trainee
D	O_{81}	O_{81}		O_{84}	O_{83}	Goal: master process 3 by year's end
E	O_{80}	O_{83}			O_{81}	Goal: master process 4 by year's end

NOTE: number indicates the year operator mastered the skill

trary, a healthy atmosphere of internal competition among the operators soon developed.

The next step was to rotate each operator's job at stated time intervals, in this case every two hours since each operation required different skills and levels of mental and physical stress. A job rotation chart was developed in advance through discussion among supervisors and operators, taking into account the skill levels, preferences, and physical condition of each operator.

In Exhibit 5.3, operators C and E are restricted to certain processes; whereas operators A and B can handle all processes. Also, as the chart indicates, operator D is being trained on process 3 by a supervisor between 10:00 A.M. and noon.

Exhibit 5.3. Example of Communicating Job Rotation Schedule

Job Rotation Chart						
Process No. / Period	**1**	**2**	**3**	**4**	**5**	**Comments**
8:00–10:00 A.M.	A	B	C	D	E	
10:00–12:00 P.M.	E	A	D*	C	B	*Operator D needs more training
1:00–3:00 P.M.	D	E	A	B	C	
3:00–5:00 P.M.	E	D	C	A	B	

The results of skill development and job rotation at this defense contractor have been very positive. Some of the major benefits are as follows:

1. Job rotation challenges most operators to set goals for developing their skills.
2. Job rotation at stated intervals (e.g., two hours, one day, etc.) gives operators an opportunity to vary their work pattern. Most operators found this refreshing, and helpful in maintaining concentration.
3. Job rotation at short intervals allows operators to use different muscles and senses, and helps prevent the development of muscle and eye strain.
4. Job rotation facilitates the sharing of skills among operators and supervisors and encourages strong teamwork.
5. As operators become more aware of the total production process, they start to help each other by communicating information on work procedures, solving operational problems, and developing improvement ideas. Each operator also starts to view the overall operation of the group as his or her area of interest.
6. As skills are shared and communication improves, the traditional forms of craftsmanship fade away and people start to develop standard work procedures.
7. As each operator develops a sense of teamwork, he or she becomes more concerned about such areas as safety, housekeeping, quality, cost, and delivery.

In summary, job rotation will not only increase the flexibility of production activities as demand changes and facilitate multiprocess handling operations, but it will also increase coordination among people and vitalize the organization as a whole.

SUMMARY

Upgrading employee skills is essential in order to compete effectively in today's business environment. While it is difficult in many cases to change from the comfortable practices of the past, this is equivalent to the entrance fee we all have to pay in order to play the game of business. We should also keep in mind that by providing oppor-

tunities for people to expand their skills, unforeseen benefits will unfold.

Since the issue of people's skills is so critical in today's businesses, we will return to this important subject later in chapters 15 and 16.

Chapter 6

Improving Processes for Productivity Gains

While the application of the concepts of flow production and multiprocess handling will substantially improve labor productivity, quality, and production lead time as well as inventory and floor space requirements, we should remember that each improvement should not be seen as an isolated event. Instead, several implications associated with the change need to be addressed simultaneously.

Accordingly, we will focus on several approaches to *process improvement* in this chapter. Managerial issues, such as job security and organizational responsibilities, and technical issues such as quality, maintenance, and scheduling will also be introduced here in preparation for a discussion of these issues later in the book.

PRINCIPLES FOR PROCESS IMPROVEMENT

Just as discipline helps in acquiring skills in sports, certain principles will help in learning the skills for process improvement more quickly. Twelve principles for process improvement are summarized in Exhibit 6.1:

Exhibit 6.1. Twelve Principles for Process Improvement

1. Organize the Workplace	(Chapter 2)
2. Develop Quick Setup	(Chapter 3)
3. Eliminate Transportation Loss	(Chapter 4)
4. Develop Fixtures for One-Touch Placement and Automatic Ejection	(Chapter 4)
5. Introduce Multiprocess Handling	(Chapter 5)
6. Synchronize Processes	(Chapter 6)
7. Use Transfer Lot Size of One	(Chapter 6)
8. Introduce *Jidoka* Concept	(Chapter 7)
9. Introduce *Poka-Yoke,* Statistical Process Control	(Chapter 7)
10. Eliminate Machine Troubles	(Chapter 8)
11. Determine Cycle Time	(Chapter 9)
12. Standardize Work Procedures	(Chapter 10)

As the exhibit indicates, process improvement involves many different disciplines. Some will be discussed later, in detail, but for now we should know that integrating these disciplines is the key to successful process improvement.

In the rest of this chapter, we will examine how some of these principles are basic to process improvement. As an example of what can be achieved from these efforts, Exhibit 6.2 summarizes the savings realized by an automotive parts manufacturer in the Midwest after applying these principles for eighteen months.

U-Shaped Lines

As a product-oriented layout is developed and operators become capable of handling multiple processes, organizing the layout in a U-shaped form often makes the most sense. (This enables operators to produce and transfer parts one piece at a time. This is called *one-piece flow production.*) As Exhibit 6.3 shows, a U-*shaped line* minimizes an operator's walking time and walking distance. There are other benefits as well.

If machines are laid out in an I- or L-shaped form, operators may feel that too much walking is tiring and they may start to operate machines in a batch production mode. This requires additional space to accumulate in-process inventories and also results in more

Exhibit 6.2. Savings Achieved in an Automotive Parts Manufacturer in the Midwest

Project	Reduction in Production Floor Space (%)	Increase in Labor Productivity (%)	Reduction of Work-In-Process (%)	Annualized Savings ($000)
A	58	44	99	99
B	71	7	99	202
C	24	20	97	50
D	37	32	99	80
E	41	56	99	220
F	5	9	98	46
G	5	15	90	50
H	20	8	96	82
I	34	31	99	50
J	17	55	86	170
K	33	38	96	87
L	85	29	99	62
M	44	21	99	94
N	46	44	99	74
O	25	42	82	85
P	36	14	99	122
Q	17	21	86	125
R	36	44	89	65
S	51	52	98	290

Total Reduction in Production Floor Space	31,000 sq. ft.		
Total Reduction of Work-in-Process		$390,000	
Total Annualized Savings			$2.1 million

Note: Saving from quality improvement is not included here, but it is estimated at over $1 million per year.

waste, such as unnecessary handling of materials, slow feedback of quality information, and longer production lead time.

But from the operators' point of view, batch processing may seem easier especially if their chief concern is to produce volume.

Exhibit 6.3. Comparison of Line Layout and Operator Walking Patterns

Exhibit 6.4. U-Shaped Line in a Small Sheet Metal Shop in Japan

PROCESS ANALYSIS FOR MULTIPLE VARIETIES OF ITEMS

Process analysis may be easy if only a few products are involved, but when a large variety of products requires materials to be moved through many and complex processes, analysis can be much more

difficult. The flow of material through the plant, however, can be simplified by following these steps.

1. *Product-quantity analysis.* To better understand the product profile, *product-quantity* (PQ) *analysis* may be conducted. This produces a profile of product items showing the relationship between production unit size and dollar volume.

Exhibit 6.5. Product-Quantity Analysis

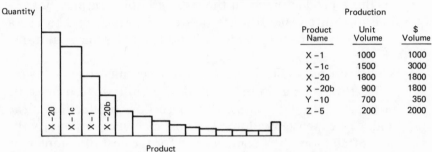

Product Name	Unit Volume	$ Volume
X – 1	1000	1000
X – 1c	1500	3000
X – 20	1800	1800
X – 20b	900	1800
Y – 10	700	350
Z – 5	200	2000

2. *Process route analysis.* The next step is to conduct a process route analysis summarizing the processes necessary for completion of each product item. (Depending on the result of PQ analysis, low-volume items may be considered separately.)

Exhibit 6.6. Process Route Analysis Sheet

Product Name	Production Volume	Sheer	Press	Brake	Weld
X – 1	1000	(1) →	(2) →	(3) →	(4)
X – 1c	1500	(1) ———————→		(2) →	(3)
X – 20	1800		(1) →	(2) →	(3)
X – 20b	900		(1) ———————→		(2)
Y – 10	700	(1) ———————→		(2) →	(3)
Z – 5	200		(1) →	(2) →	(3)

3. *Grouping.* When the process route analysis is completed, product items should be grouped according to the sequence of processes. All identical and similar processes should be grouped together.

Exhibit 6.7. Product Item Grouping

Product Name	Production Volume	Sheer	Press	Brake	Weld
X – 1c	1500	(1) ———————→		(2) →	(3)
X – 10	700	(1) ———————→		(2) →	(3)
X – 1	1000	(1) →	(2) →	(3) →	(4)
X – 20	1800		(1) →	(2) →	(3)
Z – 5	200		(1) →	(2) →	(3)
X – 20b	900		(1) ———————→		(2)

4. *Idea Generation.* Simply by following the steps described here, a number of improvement ideas will be generated. Some of the key points in developing a streamlined production flow are as follows:

- Machine capacity, process time for both hand and machine time, setup time, tool change frequency, lot size, and machine maintenance should be considered in the process of developing new machine layouts and material flows.
- For those product items in the same grouping, it may be possible to shorten the distance between processes and to use a chute, conveyor, or to carry by hand for better material transfer.
- When there are multiple machines of a certain category, a simplified flow such as in the right diagram in Exhibit 6.8 will be most desirable. Of course, one-piece flow production is the goal. The expense of adding low cost machines to simplify the flow often more than compensates for the cost of complexity.

Exhibit 6.8. Use of Dedicated Flow Concept to Simplify Flow

Before: Complex Flow—Not Dedicated After: Simple Flow—Dedicated

Note: ☐ :Work station

- In the process of developing a new machine layout, it is advisable to consult people from different disciplines—e.g., quality assurance, maintenance, production control, process engineering, industrial engineering, foremen, and operators. Marketing projections should be incorporated into the plan to allow for flexibility.

APPROACHES TO PROCESS IMPROVEMENT

The following case examples will familiarize you with approaches to process improvement activities. It should be emphasized that by sim-

ply reviewing a number of examples, one may fully grasp the process of improvement even if the situation described is not directly applicable.

Examples

Process analysis and layout change. A sporting goods manufacturer on the West Coast has been using just-in-time production techniques for over three years. Most of the machines were rearranged when the factory was converted from a process-oriented layout to a product-oriented layout. Inventory level was reduced from over two hundred days to under seventy days. Production lead time was reduced by about 90 percent on average. However, there is still vast room for improvement in this factory. Exhibit 6.9 shows one area of this factory identified as a target for further improvement.

Exhibit 6.9. Layout (Before Improvement)

In this arrangement, machines were located according to the production sequence. (In the original layout, all milling machines had been clustered away from the rest of the operation.) One operator conducted operations A through D with a production batch size of thirty units for each operation. When the painting operation was completed, another operator came to help pick up workpieces from the hanger conveyor and place them into the cart. This was also done in thirty-unit batches. The whole process took one or two days. Exhibit 6.10 describes the results of a process analysis of the existing layout.

By focusing on eliminating the wastes identified in the process analysis, an improved process was developed (see Exhibit 6.11). Exhibit 6.12 shows the layout after improvement. One-piece flow pro-

75

Exhibit 6.10. Process Analysis (Before Improvement)

Number of Steps	Description of Process	Material Status	Comments
1	▽	Storage	Too big purchasing lot size (lot size of 5 weeks)
2	⬦	Transfer by Cart	Distance: 50 ft. Batch size: 30 units
3	▽	Storage	Waste in material handling
4	Ⓐ	Milling Operation	Waste in operators watching machine operation
5	▽	Storage	Waste of inventory, material handling
6	⬦	Transfer	Waste of transportation (Distance: 15 ft)
7	▽	Storage	same as #5
8	Ⓑ	Grinding Operation	
9	▽	Storage	same as #5
10	Ⓒ	Grinding Operation	
11	⬦	Transfer	Waste of transportation (Distance: 3 ft)
12	▽	Storage	same as #5
13	Ⓓ	Grinding Operation	
14	☐	Inspection	
15	▽	Storage	same as #5
16	◯	Hanger	**Hanging position too high**
17	Ⓔ	Paint	
18	◯	Take off	
19	▽	Storage in Cart	

Note: ◯ = process

⬦ = transfer

▽ = store

☐ = inspect

Other comments:
- no clear control of production
- bad clamping method at milling machine

duction was achieved, with improvements made by rearranging the machines.

As the process analysis shows, there is no longer any waste in transportation and in-process storage. Because of the significantly shortened lead time, quality problems are quickly identified, contributing to a significant reduction in defects. Furthermore, the time

Exhibit 6.11. Process Analysis (After Improvement)

Number of Steps	Description of Process	Material Status	Comments
1	▽	Storage	Use of small container
2	Ⓐ	Milling Operation	Use of better clamping method
3	Ⓑ	Grinding	
4	Ⓒ	Grinding	
5	Ⓓ	Grinding	
6	☐	Inspection	One-Piece Flow Production
7	○	Hanger	
8	Ⓔ	Paint	
9	○	Take Off	
10	▽	Storage in Cart	

Note: ○ = process

◁▷ = transfer

▽ = store

☐ = inspect

Other comments:

• Potential to automate take-off operation

Exhibit 6.12. Layout (After Improvement)

Note: → Material Flow

previously spent by one operator assisting the other operator by taking the workpiece off the hanger can now be utilized more productively. Also the need for one cart for material transfer and one bench for temporary storage has been eliminated. A summary of the improvements is shown in Exhibit 6.13.

Exhibit 6.13. Summary of Improvement

	Before	After
In-process Inventory	30 units	1 unit
Lead time	1 to 2 days	10 minutes
Space	100 (index)	50
Labor Productivity	-	30% improvement
Quality	-	Significant improvement

"Rabbit chase". Exhibit 6.14 is a simplified layout for a machining line of a large midwestern manufacturer. The previous layout required ten people. The zig-zag material flow is indicated by arrows in the exhibit. As one can imagine, materials handling was a nuisance to operators, who spent most of their time pulling and pushing containers, picking and placing parts, and watching machines run, rather than working to add value to the product.

Exhibit 6.14. Machining Line Layout (Before Improvement)

Only a few operators handled more than one machine. Because of occasional machine problems and the lack of line balance, inventory was accumulated as a buffer between processes. The conveyor was used to accumulate in-process inventories which were stacking up on the layers of containers. This, in turn, contributed to a lack of communication or coordination between operators.

Shielded by inventories between processes, each operator conducted his work at his own pace. Because of the inventory pileups, wastes were not exposed. Occasionally, defects were found in large quantities at downstream inspection points. The feedback of such

information was slow, and often it was difficult to identify the source of defects.

This situation, with variations, is still very common in many factories. Over the years people may have assumed that they were working efficiently, but in reality, the value-added portion of their time was a small percentage of the total time they spent in the factory.

One solution to this situation is to eliminate the conveyor, place machines closer together, and conduct operations one piece at a time through all processes without accumulating inventories between the processes. Exhibit 6.15 shows two U-shaped lines with two operators following each other in each line. (This arrangement is often called "rabbit chase" in Japan.)

Exhibit 6.15. Layout (After Improvement)

With this new layout, the number of operators was reduced from ten to four, inventory was reduced by 99 percent, floor space was reduced by two-thirds, and production lead time was reduced from days to minutes. Also, unneeded inspection points were reduced, yet the defects were also reduced by 72 percent because of quick information feedback (see Exhibit 6.16). In this example, the benefit was already significant but much more substantial gains were still possible.

Exhibit 6.16. Summary of Improvement

	Before	After
No. Operators	10	4
Inventory (indexed)	100	<1
Defects (indexed)	100	28
Floor Space (indexed)	100	32

Since the number of operators required was reduced, some were then trained to do maintenance work, some were trained in statistical process control and setup operations, others were moved to new areas. Also, new business was developed when the company began to manufacture parts that had previously been purchased. People are now working together to improve quality, cost, and delivery time in a fight against competition rather than simply accepting slow death, which would have been the inevitable result.

"There is no end to improvement". In the previous examples, we reviewed basic process analysis and established a U-shaped layout with a one-piece flow production. This example, illustrates a similar process of improvement in a fabrication shop, to demonstrate that the possibilities for improvement are endless.

As shown in Exhibit 6.17, a U-shaped line was developed with two operators following each other (a "rabbit chase" arrangement). Significant gains were achieved in labor productivity. Also, most of the conveyors and in-process inventory were taken away.

A few months after the new line began operation, yet another layout was developed in response to operators' comments and further analysis of machine usage. This layout uses much less floor space and requires less walking, less inventory buildup, and no conveyor. The number of inspection benches was also reduced. One machine was freed up after a newly developed fixture was attached to another machine, thereby improving product quality.

Again, the lesson learned was that there is no end to improvement. The involvement of the operators was the key to creating a better workplace, and one conducive to further improvement. Two of the operators' suggestions were to reduce the distance between machines further, and to put an inspection bench in the middle of the U-shaped layout. Both suggestions were incorporated into the plan.

Two-piece flow production. This example of an automotive parts manufacturer is slightly different from the previous cases in that the operation uses two-piece flow production with two operators, each following the other.

Two pin racks, each holding about 2000 pieces of in-process inventory were eliminated in the new layout, freeing up about 40 per-

Exhibit 6.17. Process and Summary of Improvement

Summary of Improvement

	Before	Present	Proposed
Number of Operators	4	2	1-2
Work-in-Process (pcs.)	542	12	9
Floor Space (sq. ft.)	1075	920	560
Conveyor (ft.)	140	10	0
Number of Benches	5	3	1

Note: Process 6 was eliminated because of improved quality achieved at process 5.

cent of the previously occupied space. The major savings came from quality and labor productivity improvements, totaling more than $150,000 per year. The expense of rearranging the machines was less than $5000. (See Exhibits 6.18 and 6.19.)

(Please note that labor savings, should not result in layoffs. Rather, the surplus people are moved to new positions, often allowing a company to gain more business. The issue of job security will be discussed in Chapter 14.)

Exhibit 6.18. A Two-Piece Cycle U-Shaped Line Developed at an Automotive Parts Manufacturer

Summary of Improvement

	Before	After	Improvement
Floor space	1148 sq. ft.	720 sq. ft.	37%
In-process Inventory	4000 pcs	10 pcs	99%
Number of Operators	2.7	2	25%
Output per Person	168	217	23%
Scrap	100 (indexed)	26 (indexed)	74%

Incorporation of a feeder line. In a household goods manufacturing company on the West Coast, a U-shaped layout was developed in the feeder line as shown in Exhibit 6.20. However, the linkage between the feeder line and the assembly line was weak and there were several problems associated with this arrangement:

1. Production information was communicated separately to the feeder line and the final assembly line. As a result, the feeder

Exhibit 6.19. U-Shaped Layout at an Automotive Parts Manufacturer in the Midwest

Exhibit 6.20. Line Balance Between Main Assembly Line and Feeder Line

line tended to overproduce some parts while experiencing shortages in others.

2. In general, too much inventory accumulated between the feeder line and the final assembly operation, creating double or triple handling of materials, and a lack of close communication between them.

3. Since the feeder line was treated as an isolated island, operators were sometimes underutilized without being able to help in other operations.

To address these problems, improvements were made as shown in Exhibit 6.20. After this improvement, the feeder line was connected to the final assembly line, improving the communication of production information to the feeder line operator, who was able to identify the product type from instructions attached to the workpiece on the final assembly line.

With this arrangement, the operator was able to produce the subassembly component just in time to meet the final assembly schedule. Inventories that previously built up between the feeder line and the final assembly line were totally eliminated together with the necessary space required to hold them.

Other benefits of this new arrangement were improved labor productivity and increased flexibility to cope with volume changes. By combining the work content of the operations in the feeder line with that of the final assembly line, one position was eliminated from this area. Also, as production volume varies, jobs can now be combined much more easily and the staffing requirements can be adjusted more readily than before.

Tying an isolated process into the mainstream processes. Even though the use of small equipment helps the development of production flow in the factory, there may be cases where equipment must be physically located away from the main process flow. Even if it is difficult to incorporate this equipment into the flow of the production process because of the expense required to move it, or for safety, hygiene, dust, heat, quality, or other reasons, we must continue to seek new ideas to ensure a smooth production flow.

In Exhibit 6.21, process 4 is located away from the other six processes. As a result, production flow is divided into three groups (i.e., processes 1 through 3; process 4; and processes 5 through 7). This results in a lack of communication, coordination, and cooperation among the people involved. But by introducing the *kanban* concept, this situation can be alleviated. (The kanban concept will be described in more detail in Chapter 11.)

First, as the operator completes process 3, the finished parts will be stored in a container next to the process (location A). After the operator in process 4 consumes this part, the empty container at

Exhibit 6.21. Use of Kanban Concept in Tying Isolated Processes

Note:
1, 3: transfer of
 finished parts
2, 4: return of empty
 container

process 4 is returned to location A. In exchange for the empty container, another container with finished parts from process 3 is moved to location B for use at process 4. Here, the number of containers is fixed and they are used only between processes 3 and 4.

Similarly, as the operator completes process 4, the finished parts will be stored in the container located at the process (location C). After the operator in process 5 consumes this part, the empty container at process 5 is returned to location C for refill. In exchange for the empty container, the container with finished parts from process 4 is then moved to location D for use at process 5. The number of containers is fixed and used only between processes 4 and 5.

When only one operator is doing work on both processes 3 and 5, for example, one-piece flow production will be conducted simply by leaving the finished part from process 3 in the container at location A and picking up the part from the container at location D. Then the operator will finish process 5 and go back to process 3 to start the cycle again.

In this arrangement, where a fixed number of containers is used to link processes 3, 4, and 5, the isolated process can thus be linked into the mainstream of processes. Please also note that the isolated process can be tied to more than one line by designating containers to serve as the link. Of course, the timing of container transfers and decisions about how many containers to use will require some careful planning. However, the simple concept described here can help to link the processes and develop a smooth flow of material with minimum involvement of production control people.

Examples from Japanese Factories

The following examples are taken from Japanese companies with ten to fifteen years of devoted efforts in process improvement. They are

very advanced in terms of effectively using and improving available equipment.

One-piece flow production in a welding shop. In a welding shop, for example, when a number of parts are combined to form a product, the development of a synchronized flow throughout the processes may appear to be difficult. As shown in Exhibit 6.22, however, it is yet possible to accomplish this in a layout where both spot and arc welding machines coexist.

Exhibit 6.22. One-Piece Flow Production in a Welding Shop

Layout and Process Chart

Note:

At the process 2, parts from processes 1 and 3 are spot-welded together. Similarly, at process 8, parts from processes 7 and 9 are spot-welded together. Other processes represent punch brake, spot and arc welding, and so forth.

The shop shown here uses eighteen machines and eight operators to produce about eight hundred automotive panels per day. The company is affiliated with one of the major automobile manufacturers and has sales of less than $5 million annually.

In this example, each automotive panel has four major components. All processes are synchronized at a 40-second cycle time. That means that a significant delay (e.g., 5 seconds or more caused by one operator) will halt the entire operation. For a small delay (e.g., 3 seconds or less) a neighboring operator can assist in the operation. (This arrangement is called a *relay zone* since neighboring operators assist one another at the borders of their areas of responsibilty just as in a track relay.)

As a part of their ongoing improvement activities, this factory recently held a two-day improvement session to which several other suppliers were also invited. The objective was to make the production process more flexible to meet volume changes and to reduce the number of operators by one. The participants accomplished both objectives: they further improved the production-line layout and acted upon over fifty suggestions generated during the two days. The quest for improvement is never-ending.

U-*Shaped line in a sheet metal shop.* Generally speaking, quite a few people think of their shops as job shops, and this is typically so in a sheet metal shop. By conducting PQ analysis and process route analysis, however, we often find that this is not the case.

Exhibit 6.23 shows the use of a U-shaped line for different product families. With this arrangement, a good combination of machine capacity utilization and operator's time utilization was achieved while preserving a smooth material flow.

The complexity associated with machine-hopping is resolved by using a traffic-light concept—that is, the operator should follow the machines with green lights and skip the operation of those with yellow lights.

U-*Shaped line in a press shop.* This example of improvement occurred more than ten years ago at one of Toyota's affiliated companies. The company had used a straight-line layout with one operator to a machine, where each operator conducted his work at his own pace. As a result, there were high levels of in-process inventory

Exhibit 6.23. U-Shaped Line with Different Patterns of Material Flows

tied with the imbalance of the processes. Also, a lot of time was wasted in pick and place, and in watching the machines run.

By synchronizing each process, improving material transfer, eliminating in-process inventory, and conducting one-piece flow production, three people could achieve the same production volume originally done by seven.

SUMMARY

By combining the concepts of flow production and upgraded operator skills, production processes can become much more streamlined and significant productivity gains can be achieved. Furthermore, production lead time is reduced and quality level is increased substantially.

Because of the benefits associated with a streamlined production flow, the production control function becomes easier. On the other hand, careful attention is required to monitor the processes in such areas as quality and machine operating status.

Since different processes are tightly linked, problems are exposed much more quickly. At the same time, the system becomes more susceptible to sudden disruptions. This is especially true in the early

Exhibit 6.24. Improvement at Press Line in a Japanese Automotive Parts Manufacturer

Improvement Achieved		
	Before	After
In-process Inventory	1800 pcs.	7 pcs.
Number of Operators	7	3

phase of improved operations when many changes are necessary. Consequently, potential problems should be predicted as much as possible before the improvement takes place. Also, better monitoring and problem-solving abilities should be developed as discussed in the next chapter.

Chapter 7

Strengthening Our Nerves and Muscles

Even if layout, equipment, and operators' skills are improved, substantial gains will not be achieved without a reliable system of feedback. Quick detection of problems or failure to meet expected standards is especially important in taking corrective action in a timely manner.

In order to develop such a feedback system, however, it may be worthwhile to compare the operations in our factory to that of a healthy human body where nerves and muscles are well coordinated. The human body has a reflexive nervous system that responds almost instantly so that muscles will react to such things as touching a hot plate. In addition, the body's autonomic nervous system responds to such activities as eating or exercising where the stomach and heart muscles respond autonomously.

Contrasting this, in our production activities we often depend heavily on our brain power. However, instead of generating stacks of computer printouts filled with numbers or relying on the manuals and reference materials that pile up on our file cabinets, we need to develop and utilize our reflexive and autonomic nerves and muscles to take care of problems on the shop floor as soon as they arise.

In this chapter, we will discuss the application of such an idea and give examples. As in the case of doing exercises to develop our bodies in preparation for sports competition, we need to build up our ability to take appropriate action by introducing an effective feedback system and developing teamwork among people.

JIDOKA (AUTONOMATION)

Automated machines are often used in today's factories. The operators of these machines do not have to use their hands; by simply pushing a switch, the machines will work by themselves.

This is an advance from the very labor-intensive machines of the old days. However, most automated machines do have limitations. They do not usually detect problems while they are running, nor can they use judgment to determine when to stop operating.

As a result, operators need to watch machines run. But having operators watch these machines run does not add value to the product. Rather, it adds cost to the product. If we can eliminate this wasteful time by separating operators from machines, then operators can handle more work. To do this, however, we need to upgrade the machines' capabilities. When abnormal conditions arise, such as defects, tool damage, or a lack of parts supply, the machine should stop its operation and dispatch a signal for the operator's help. The machine should have intelligence to detect these abnormal conditions in order to inform operators to take appropriate action.

Jidoka (autonomation) is a concept developed in Japan to provide machines with the autonomous capability to use judgment. Without this concept, a machine may *move* by itself, but it may not *work* for you.

Exhibit 7.1 Evolution Toward Jidoka (Autonomation)

Old Days	Pre-Jidoka	Jidoka

Operator handles a large part of the work

Operator watches machine operation most of the time

Obsolete operator is assigned to a greater challange

Example: Shearing

In a shearing operation, the operator stood idle while the machine was running. In order to better utilize the operator's time, the re-

quirements for unmanned machine operation were investigated and the following improvements were made:

1. A limit switch was installed to check the need for replenishing coil. When the coil is about to run out, a light panel (or *Andon* in Japanese) lights up and a speaker sounds so that the operator can prepare the next coil.
2. A counter was installed in the machine to monitor the number of strokes. When the required amount of material is completed, the light panel and the buzzer signal the operator.
3. A limit switch and timer were installed to monitor the machine troubles. When the limit switch is on for more than the prescribed time period, the machine stops automatically and the light panel and the buzzer signal the operator.

Exhibit 7.2. Application of Jidoka in a Shearing Operation

With these improvements in place, labor productivity increased significantly. The operator is now able to concentrate on other jobs, such as quality assurance, and other higher value added operations.

Other Examples

- A plastic injection moulding machine has a small and a large hopper. When the level of resin in the small hopper gets low, a detector emits a signal to feed resin from a large hopper until the amount of resin reaches the proper level.
- When a problem develops in a machine tool (e.g., drill, tap), a detector (e.g., electric current, limit switch, etc.) stops the machine and emits a signal to inform operators about the abnormal condition.

- As indicated in Exhibit 7.3, limit switches or kanban squares can control the inventory levels between processes, thereby eliminating waste associated with overproduction.

Exhibit 7.3. Application of Jidoka for Inventory Control

Electric Kanban

Note: When there is a certain amount of inventory accumulated between machines, the limit switch will signal to automatically stop the upstream process.

Note: When there is a product in the square, the operator in the upstream process should stop production. This makes sense because the downstream (i.e., customer) process is not requiring the next product to work on yet.

LINE STOP CONCEPT

The jidoka concept addresses the point that by putting man's intelligence into machines, operators can be separated from machine operation. This makes better utilization of the operators' time possible and more rapid troubleshooting by exposing abnormal conditions for everyone to notice.

This concept points out that establishing strong production capability requires well-disciplined approaches. Whenever a process is disturbed, we need to identify the problem by stopping the process, resolve the problem, and regain the streamlined flow as early as possible. Otherwise, the same problem may haunt us forever.

The jidoka concept applies not only to machine operations, but also to line operations. For example, an assembly line may use conveyors to transfer workpieces. Whenever there is trouble in the op-

eration, it should be reported to the line supervisor so that corrective action can be taken immediately. But when a major problem is exposed and corrective action is not taken in time, the whole line will stop until it receives appropriate management attention.

The sequence of events for an assembly line stop may be as follows:

1. The operator will push the trouble button to get a supervisor's assistance when he finds a problem or he cannot conduct his work on time as prescribed in his work instructions. (This is an application of the relay zone concept, where the operator and his supervisor form a team.)
2. If the supervisor can help solve the problem in time, the line will keep moving. However, if the problem is not solved in time, the line will stop at the point where the impact on other operators is minimal. (For safety-related problems, the line may be stopped instantly by pushing the emergency button.)
3. If the line stops, the time to recover the line will vary depending upon the degree of the problem. Time and duration of the line stop, location, reasons, and other comments may be recorded so that people can think of ways to eliminate line stops.

Typically, an andon light is used to signal these events—perhaps a yellow light for requesting assistance with a problem and a red light for line stoppage when the problem is not resolved in time.

One important point to remember is that we should not fear the line stop. Rather, we should even encourage the line stop in order to expose problems.

ANDON (TROUBLE LIGHTS)

Generally, in a factory where improvement activities are dormant, we find that differences between normal and abnormal conditions are barely discernible. When there is a problem, it may be obscured by a large amount of inventory, the lack of monitoring and timely feedback systems, or operators' failure to accept responsibility for it.

On the other hand, in a well-managed factory, improvement projects are pursued actively and problems are exposed quickly so that corrective action can be taken. This is fundamental to good management. But abnormal conditions and problems need to be ob-

vious enough to catch people's attention. Andon is used as a tool to do this.

Andon means "lantern" in Japanese. Just as a lantern may guide people walking in the dark, an andon light helps expose abnormal conditions in the factory.

Because of the emphasis on visual methods for quick information transfer, the practice is called *"management by sight,"* or *"visual control."*

Andon lights, buzzers, and video cameras facilitate information transfer without delay. When factory operations are linked by these means, the factory functions similar to our reflexive muscle system. Corrective action is taken immediately, just as our muscles pull our hand away when we touch a hot plate.

Examples

- When there is a problem in the assembly operation such as defects, a lack of parts, or machine trouble, the operator presses the trouble button to attract a supervisor's attention, and a yellow light flashes. If the problem is not solved promptly, the line may stop at a prescribed spot and a red light will be turned on automatically. If the line is long with many operators, a large light panel may be used to display the whole process, with numbers corresponding to each process (see Exhibit 7.4).
- In order to supply parts to different areas of the factory, andon may be used to inform the material handler of the location for delivery. For example, when a part inventory needs to be replenished, the operator will push a button. When the andon light appears, the material handler brings parts to the required

Exhibit 7.4. Use of Lights to Communicate Problems

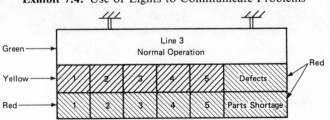

95

location. This is similar to hiring a limousine that comes at your command. Another application is similar to a bus that follows an established route and schedule. Parts are supplied at a certain cycle to satisfy the perceived need of the operators. In such a case, andon lights may be located at multiple points.

- Andon is also used to indicate the status of machine operations. In such a case, red may indicate a machine breakdown or quality problem, and yellow may mean a setup operation or parts supply (see Exhibit 7.5).
- In order to indicate the progress of a particular operation (especially a lengthy one, e.g., more than ten minutes), andon may be used to monitor elapsed time. The operator is then able to monitor the operation easily while performing additional work.

Exhibit 7.5. Andon Lamp Indicating Machine Operating Status in a Japanese Injection-Moulding Shop

Note: Arrow indicates location of andon lamp.

PRODUCTION CONTROL BOARDS

As andon is used to expose abnormal conditions, a *production control board* is used to visually convey actual production activities as

contrasted to the production schedule. Some people may think it is useless to develop schedules because they must be changed so frequently. Others may think that recording performance means tighter control or strict supervision. These are big mistakes!

We need to emphasize the *PDCA cycle—plan, do, check, action*—as prescribed in the total quality control concept. That is simply to (1) develop a plan, and (2) conduct work as planned, then (3) check results for appropriateness, and (4) analyze and take action when there is a need for further correction. This cycle enables us to develop better control over our environment, serve our customers better, and strive to create viability in business.

The production control board is one of the tools to aid us in doing this. A typical board is shown in Exhibit 7.6. Its purpose is to compare achievement to the plan and make discrepancies between the two visible to everyone. A comment column helps to identify problem areas requiring corrective action.

Exhibit 7.6. Production Control Board

Time	Plan		Actual		Comments
8:00-9:00AM	60*	60**	50*	50**	no material
9:00-10:00	60	120	60	110	
10:10-11:00	50	170	50	160	
11:00-12:00PM	60	230	60	220	
1:00-2:00	60	290	55	275	fixture problem
2:00-3:00	60	350	70	345	
3:10-4:00	50	400	48	393	machine trouble
4:00-5:00	60	460	67	460	

Note: ◯ (red mark) indicates low performance
 *:production volume per period
 **:cumulative production volume

With the production control board in place (typically at the end of the line), many supervisors have found that production plans have not been followed by line people because of a lack of communication, lack of parts, or some other reason. The board pinpointed these problems and supervisors could take appropriate action to remedy the problems.

Exhibit 7.7. Production Control Board in a Japanese Automotive Parts Manufacturer

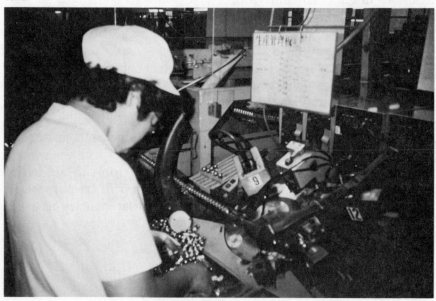

Our discussions about the importance of such concepts as leveled schedules, cycle time, and standardized work in Chapters 9 and 10 will make it clear that practicing this rather simple discipline on our shop floor is instrumental in achieving a smooth production flow. While we have studied here the benefits of a production control board, even the time to write production information on the board may be viewed as waste, especially after vast improvements in the factory have been made. We need to understand *why* we do certain things instead of just doing them out of habit. The point is that even a powerful technique needs to be continuously reevaluated and improved for the better.

POKA-YOKE (FOOLPROOF MECHANISMS)

For each of us engaged in manufacturing activities, one of the most important responsibilities is to deliver defect-free products to the next process (our customer). If we waste time in finding defects and dealing with them, the cost to the company is very high; and if we do not control our practices well, the company may not be able to maintain its market position.

Some may think that a strong inspection department is the best way to handle the situation. If we think about it more carefully, however, we realize that end-of-line inspection cannot ensure 100 percent quality. Unless we can develop a low-cost method to ensure 100 percent of the product, 100 percent quality will not be possible.

Exhibit 7.8 illustrates the importance of ensuring quality at the source. The longer the delay in discovering a problem, the higher the cost of recovery. Therefore, it makes sense to control the situation where the work is done, that is, at the most upstream operation if not at the product design stage.

Poka-yoke is a Japanese word translated as "foolproof mechanism." Poka-yoke helps operators work easily, and at the same time it eliminates troubles associated with defects, safety, mistakes in operation, and so on without requiring the operators' undue attention.

Even if an operator makes a mistake, poka-yoke will prevent defects or machine stops. The key to achieving 100 percent quality is, therefore, to prevent defects at the source and not to deliver a defective product to the next process. This should significantly reduce inspection time because inspectors will not have to spend time inspecting already guaranteed products.

In order to benefit from the application of poka-yoke, it is recommended that poka-yoke ideas be shared by many, especially among those in similar operations. The ideas should be developed not only by those on the factory floor but product designers. Also, poka-yoke ideas should be considered in new machine purchases and incorporated in new process designs.

Exhibit 7.8. Identifying Defects at the Source Lowers Costs

Defects Found at:	Own Process	Next Process	End of Line	Final Inspection	End user's hand
Cost to the Company:	$	$	$	$	$
Impact to the Company:	• Very minor	• Minor delay	• Rework	• Significant rework	• Warranty cost
			• Reschedule of work	• Delay in delivery	• Administrative cost
				• Additional inspection	• Reputation
					• Loss of market share

Examples

- Attach a fixture to the machine so that the operator will not attach workpieces in the wrong direction (see Exhibit 7.9). Simply by introducing this idea, a midwestern company has saved hundands of thousands of dollars in a year.

Exhibit 7.9. Fixture Used as Poka-Yoke

- Use counters to detect the number of welding operations and compare it with the standard. If the number does not match, an andon light will be turned on or a buzzer will sound.
- Use a limit switch to monitor the procedure. If it is performed incorrectly, the machine will not start to operate (see Exhibit 7.10).
- Use color coding to distinguish between similar parts: e.g., right is blue; left is yellow.

Exhibit 7.10. Limit Switch Used as Poka-Yoke

Example: Poka-Yoke in a Printed Circuit Assembly Shop

At a telecommunications equipment manufacturer on the West Coast, operators were hand-loading the electronic components on printed circuit boards. This was followed by a wave soldering operation. Occasionally, a certain capacitor was placed in the wrong direction, resulting in significant rework when such defects were found at the functional test area.

In order to eliminate such mistakes, a young operator came up with the idea of using a template such as that shown in Exhibit 7.11. With this template, the direction of the capacitor and the parts numbers are easily identified. Templates of this kind were prepared for each type of printed circuit board.

Exhibit 7.11. Use of a Plastic Template to Prevent Misloading of Electronic Components

Note: Arrow indicates the direction of component to be loaded

The benefit was invaluable, not only from a dollar savings and a production scheduling point of view, but also because of the favorable impact on morale for the rest of the factory organization. People in this organization are sharing these good ideas through meetings, plant newsletters, memos and wall posters.

QUALITY AT THE SOURCE

While poka-yoke or foolproof mechanisms can eliminate defects, further consideration must also be given to the process capability of machines where numerous factors can affect the product quality. For example, how can we foolproof the outer diameter of critical machining parts or solderability of a printed circuit board so that they are always within specification?

In a practical sense, we can define process capability as "the capability determined by the degree of scatter or dispersion of product quality parameters." If we want to guarantee the quality to the customer at the source, we need to develop a reliable process capability. To do this, several steps need to be followed. First, the quality pa-

rameters over time should be monitored by such method as the run chart shown in Exhibit 7.12.

Exhibit 7.12. Example of Time History of Quality Parameter on Run Chart

Quality Parameter

Upper Specification Limit (S$_u$)

Break

Tolerance

Lower Specification Limit (S$_L$)

Time

Then the scatter in the collected data needs to be analyzed to determine the potential causes. Typically, man, machine, method, and material (the 4 Ms) or their subcategories are analyzed to find out the cause of scatter.

Exhibit 7.13. Cause and Effect Diagram for Increasing Process Capability

Man	Machine	
Method	Material	Process Capability (effect)

(cause)

In practice, machine capability may be separated from the capabilities of the other 3 Ms (man, method, and material) because of its different characteristics. For example, Exhibit 7.14 illustrates process capability in relation to the level of machine and other capabilities.

In the exhibit, both Case A and Case B show the same process capability as measured by the magnitude of scatter. (Please note that the bell-shaped curve indicates the frequency distribution of measurement results where 6 σ (sigma) will cover 99.74 percent of all the measured data.) Nonetheless, Case B indicates that there were some changes at time t$_1$ when a tool change or an adjustment of operating

Exhibit 7.14. Relationship Between Process Capability and Machine Capability

Case A Case B

Note: The distinction of machine capability from process capability as depicted here was originally developed by Katsuo Aoki in the proceedings of the International Conference on Productivity and Quality Improvement, Tokyo, 1982.

parameter might have taken place. Therefore, studies should be focused on man, material, or method changes which might have taken place at around time t_1. The machine capability itself is unlikely to change suddenly. On the other hand, Case A indicates that the machine capability needs to be studied more closely than other potential causes. Consequently, manufacturing process engineers should focus their efforts on Case A to increase the machine capability, while production people should focus their efforts on Case B in order to control the process toward the center of the tolerance or the optimal point.

With this type of process capability analysis, we can single out the cause of scatter and narrow the scatter itself to improve process capability. Once the improvement is realized, a new standard should be established so that process capability will not slip back to the previous level. It should be obvious from this exercise that an inspection-based quality assurance approach cannot be as effective as one focused on increasing process capability at the source.

The three phases for increasing process capability are depicted in Exhibit 7.15.

First Phase: The process is not under control. Typically, inspectors are located at the end of the line, the production lot size is big, and the production lead time is long. Also, communication among inspectors, production people, maintenance crew, and others is almost nonexistent. Nobody feels responsible for product quality. There is a lot of scrap and rework generated.

Second Phase: Improvements have been made such that a number of parameters have been identified and certain standards estab-

Exhibit 7.15. Increasing Process Capability

Note: S_u: Upper Specification Limit
S_L: Lower Specification Limit

lished. Also, communication is now better. There are, however, scrap and rework still generated in this phase.

Third Phase: The process is under control. Production people, quality assurance people, maintenance crews, manufacturing process engineers, product design engineers, and others each understand their role and work together as a team. There is no scrap or rework generated anymore.

Example 1

In a midwestern automobile factory, the operators and the inspectors had two different job categories. After the parts were produced, the inspectors came by and billed out the "inspected" materials so that the trucking people could pick them up later for transfer to the next process.

As kanban methods were introduced in this factory, this inspection procedure became an obvious problem. (See Chapter 11 for an explanation of kanban.) When the trucking people from the downstream process came to pick up the materials under the kanban operating rules, they often found that materials were not ready.

In order to solve this problem, the operators were made responsible for billing out the material. Consequently the inspectors can now spend much more time in assuring the process capability within the line rather than at the end of the line. Defects are found earlier and are not transferred to downstream operations in large quantities.

The result of this procedural change has been substantial to this 2500-employee factory. Not only has the trucking people's problem been resolved, but the quality level has improved significantly. Exhibit 7.16 measures two representative improvements in 100 or more lines where the new procedure was instituted. While the level of defects is still high, millions of dollars of savings are now expected from this procedural change across the factory.

Exhibit 7.16. Benefits Achieved from Improved Inspection Procedures

Example 2

In the same factory, a procedure was developed some time ago to reduce the need for end-of-line inspection. This is called a standard gauging frequency procedure. One piece is gauged at a certain interval—for example, every fifty pieces—to assure that the measurement is within tolerance, such as 2.7175 plus or minus 0.0015 inches. If the measurement is close to the specification limit, the operator

adjusts the position of the fixture so that the measured parameter fits within the tolerance.

Following this procedure, the operator would adjust to the mean value as shown in Exhibit 7.17 (point A to point B in the exhibit). Often, however, the operator used his judgment to overadjust, to compensate for tool wear or thermal expansion of the tool (point A to point C in Exhibit 7.17). The problem was that the operator's decision was based on the measurement of one piece. While this procedure was used for many years in this factory and applied to about a hundred machines, nobody every questioned whether or not one piece was a good enough information base.

Exhibit 7.17. Run Chart for the First Fifty Pieces

After reviewing the procedure, however, an experiment was made and a run chart was developed where each of the 200 pieces was measured to determine the process capability. The results, shown in Exhibit 7.18, indicate that the process was actually well within the tolerance, at least for the 200 pieces measured in this analysis. Obviously, if the machine had been adjusted at point A in the exhibit, it would have generated a lot of rework or scrap.

Exhibit 7.18. Continuation of Run Chart

Why did nobody question this seemingly erroneous practice for so many years? Is it because of inattention to detail, or irresponsible operators, foremen, inspectors, and quality engineers? Or, is it the high inventory level and unsteady flow of materials? While this prac-

tice may be viewed as one exceptional case, I would argue the point here that no world-class manufacturer would stand for any defect in its factory. We should question persistently the reasons why defects occur and question ourselves: How can we develop appropriate nerves and muscles across our organization to detect or expose problems that require immediate attention?

After process capability analysis and tool life study, the sampling procedure was modified in this factory to inspect two to three pieces every hour for most machines instead of one in every fifty units. The savings from this change was estimated at $2 to $3 million every year.

While the savings are large, should this be the end of improvement? No, we must not stop here. Instead, a series of questions still need to be asked: "Why do we need inspection?," "What are the causes of scatter?," "How can we control the causes of scatter?," and so forth. There is no end to improvement.

VISUAL CONTROL

As the examples of line stop and poka-yoke demonstrate, the jidoka concept can be used to develop a system of autonomous control that requires the least possible supervision.

Yet whenever an abnormal condition exists, the system will give a signal requiring that timely corrective action be taken. The system thus functions like a reflexive muscle in the human body.

In order to develop such a system, andon, kanban, production control boards, and the like are used to facilitate the transfer of important information as quickly as possible. (Please see Chapter 11 for the description of kanban.) These are, in effect, forms of just-in-time information transfer in the factory. Because of their visual nature, these means are called "visual control" tools.

Exhibit 7.19. Visual Control

When there is something deviating from the standard,
it should be made obvious to anyone so that corrective
action can be taken.

Examples

Identification of operating conditions. Meters, gauges, valves, and the like may be marked to indicate the normal operating conditions so that anyone can understand them. Pressure meters may be color coded to indicate the normal condition; valves may be tagged with a card indicating the normal position. Furthermore, the responsible person's name and phone number may be posted so that anyone noticing a problem can immediately report it (see Exhibit 7.20).

Figure 7.20. Visual Control Applied to Maintain Standard Operation

Pressure gauge Valve

Housekeeping. When tools are stored in different locations according to individual preference, confusion and associated loss of time will result when several people have to use them. Supervisors, operators, management, and staff people from related fields should develop housekeeping procedures for everyone to follow. For example, if a tool is missing at the end of a day's operation, everyone should be made aware of it, and a search should be initiated (see Exhibit 7.21).

Figure 7.21. Visual Control Applied in Workplace Organization

Wrench Hammer Screwdriver Pliers

Kanban, parts storage area. The same principle can be used to indicate predetermined inventory levels, storage locations, and so on. Inventory levels may be controlled by using kanban cards and/or a maximum height indicator in the storage area. Storage location may be addressed just like the mailing address, color coded and noted on kanban.

Exhibit 7.22. Visual Control Applied for Ease of Material Handling

Parts storage Parts transfer

When andon is used for multiple lines, unique sounds or music may be used for each line along with andon to inform people of the status of the line. While this is not a *visual* means, it serves the purpose of visual control.

Exhibit 7.23. Visual Control Applied to Convey Information

Andon Speaker

Recognition/information feedback. The visual control idea can also be used to give recognition or quick feedback to employees. When we better understand the need for involving people in developing an efficient production process, we may consider the increased use of visual methods (e.g., displays—see Exhibit 7.24). The idea is

109

Exhibit 7.24 Example of Information on Displays

Machine layout	Map indicating poka-yoke
Job rotation plan	Awards for suggestions, etc.
Operator's attendance list	Housekeeping evaluation sheet
Vacation plan	Improvement activity status
Control charts	Recent case improvement
Standard work sheet	Targets and status charts for productivity,
Oiling points	quality, etc.
Safety check points	Setup charts

Exhibit 7.25. Use of Charts to Communicate Quality Data

History of Defects Produced by Different Shifts in a Canadian Company

to develop a visual and open management system which is self-explanatory even for visitors who are unfamiliar with plant activities.

In a Canadian company, a simple chart was posted to show operators the quality of performance by each shift. Shift A was found to be the best of all four shifts in terms of producing the fewest defects. With management paying more attention to defects, increased healthy internal competition, and the help of staff people for better maintenance and use of poka-yoke (foolproof mechanisms), the defect rates were reduced from 7.2 to 0.1 percent in one year.

A foreman mentioned to me that even before he posted the newest chart, there were already six people surrounding him, curious to see the performance for the current period. This instance shows that people really *are* interested in their performance. In a way the chart is similar to a scoreboard at a baseball game. The scoreboard gives us information on how the teams are doing. Without it, there may be more confusion and less interest in the game.

Exhibit 7.26 is a picture of a skill development chart in a Japanese automobile parts manufacturer. This chart is displayed in a corner of the factory showing pictures of employees, the skills they have mastered, and the date they mastered them. While there is con-

Exhibit 7.26. Skill Development Chart in a Japanese Automobile Parts Manufacturer

siderable potential to be gained through this type of openness in information sharing, the company's culture and the people's feeling about such disclosures should be considered before the practices are implemented.

SUMMARY

By utilizing our creativity and practicing such techniques as jidoka, andon, production control boards, poka-yoke, statistical process control, and visual control, factory operations become much more tightly linked with better communication, and problem-solving activities are enhanced at the source. As the entire production process becomes more efficient the contribution of these techniques becomes more important. We should try to expose problems and take corrective actions as quickly and as effectively as possible.

In a way, these activities can be compared to the nervous and muscular systems in a healthy human body which can respond readily to environmental changes. The point is to develop a self-controlled, decentralized system that does not flood the central brain with outdated information for processing. For this purpose, everybody's involvement becomes most important.

Chapter 8

Aiming for Zero Machine Trouble

A common missing link in achieving world-class manufacturing status is the lack of attention to maintenance activities. On the one hand, several sophisticated computerized maintenance programs have been developed to serve the purpose. However, without the combined efforts of operators, management, maintenance crews, and other support people, company-wide productive maintenance will not be achieved.

Just as quality should be controlled at the source rather than by inspection, zero machine breakdowns can only be assured at the source—that is, at the machine—but not by the fire-fighting mode of maintenance activities. Because of the heavy dependence on the operators' usage of machines as well as their ability to sense problems before serious machine breakdowns occur, operator involvement is a crucial step in achieving trouble-free operations.

In this chapter, the fundamental principles of machine maintenance activities are discussed. In order for a company to survive ever intensifying competition, maintenance activities should definitely be incorporated in the pursuit of manufacturing excellence.

PREVENTIVE MAINTENANCE

In order to be competitive in manufacturing, all machine breakdowns and troubles should be eliminated. Machines should be main-

113

tained to achieve a 100 percent on-demand utilization rate for immediate use as required by the next process.

The typical problems observed in factories, however, are that maintenance crews are busy coping with sudden machine breakdowns, and foregoing necessary work in fixing freewheeling, loose bolts, and the like, whereas operators think the machine breakdowns and troubles are not their responsibility.

How can we change this situation to aim for zero failure, zero trouble, and minimum waste? Exhibit 8.1 shows an approach to preventing machine breakdowns and trouble.

Exhibit 8.1. How to Prevent Machine Breakdowns and Trouble

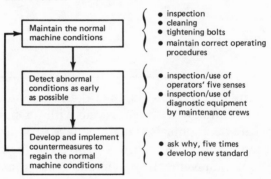

One of the basic points here is the realization that people themselves are the cause of problems. Machines do not create problems by themselves; rather, people let machines break down, for example, by forgetting to oil or tighten bolts or by leaving machines dirty. We call this forced deterioration.

We should also realize that even though machines are getting more and more sophisticated and capable, their basic function does not change. The role of people becomes more important as machines become more complex.

A closer look at a typical factory operation will reveal that a number of factors contribute to machine trouble (see Exhibit 8.2).

Over the years, we have found that the major difficulty in achieving minimum waste machine operation is the elimination of chronic problems. The causes of suddenly exposed problems are easier to determine than those of chronic problems since the relationship between cause and effect is generally clear. Chronic problems, on the

Exhibit 8.2. Factors Leading to Machine Trouble

Machines	Operators	Maintenance Crews
Dirty machine	Not concerned about dirty machine	Replace or repair parts, but do not question why trouble occurred
Dirty oiler		
Flooded oil pan	Make mistakes in operation	
Oil leakage		Do not instruct or work with operators on basic/ easy maintenance job
Empty oiler	Have no knowledge of inspection	
Heated motor		
Noisy motor	Cannot conduct easy maintenance	Do not effectively communicate with operators
Vibration		
Scattered chips	Lack knowledge of machine itself—oiling, tool change, parts change, adjustment, etc.	Focus efforts on major urgent troubles, and forget about dealing with quality-related problems and loss of machine speed
Difficulties in inspection		
Dirty floor	Do not ask for help even when problem exists	
Unnecessary goods		Consider machine deterioration as unavoidable
Lack of organization	Consider production more important than good machine maintenance	
		Seek solutions in new machines or new technologies rather than in available resources
	Do not have control over machines	

Exhibit 8.3. Machine Problems and their Countermeasures

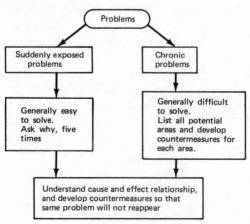

other hand, may not be eliminated even after implementing several countermeasures (see Exhibit 8.3).

Since chronic problems usually have more than one cause, we need to look at *all* potential problem areas (see Exhibit 8.4 on five major causes of machine troubles). It therefore becomes necessary to develop countermeasures for all potential causes.

Exhibit 8.4. Five Major Causes of Machine Troubles

1. Failure to maintain fundamental machine requirements, e.g., housekeeping, oiling, bolt tightening, etc.
2. Failure to maintain correct operating conditions, e.g., temperature, vibration, pressure, speed, torque, etc.
3. Lack of skills, e.g., operator's mis-operation, maintenance crew's errors.
4. Deterioration, e.g., of bearings, gears, fixtures, etc.
5. Design deficiency, e.g., materials, dimension, etc.

Note: Generally, a combination of these elements causes machine troubles.

Experience shows that most machine problems are not solved in the office. We should spend our time on the shop floor facing the problem directly. Typically, this is a much better approach than looking for easy solutions and taking a trial-and-error approach.

The Five "Whys"

The process of questioning should be persistent, so that problems do not recur. As Taiichi Ohno of Toyota comments, if we ask "why" five times, we may be able to capture the true cause of a problem. (See Exhibit 8.5.)

Exhibit 8.5. Five Whys

Problem: Malfunction of digital controller for NC machine

Why ⟶ Defective printed circuit board
 Why ⟶ Lack of cooling
 Why ⟶ Lack of air
 Why ⟶ Lack of pressure
 Why ⟶ Dust on filter

Solution: Clean filter every month

Maintaining Normal Conditions

While developing countermeasures is important in eliminating the cause of a problem, one of the key points in preventing machine trouble is to maintain the normal operating conditions. This can be done effectively by increasing our ability to identify the initial symptoms of machine trouble as early as possible (see Exhibit 8.6). The operator's role is thus very important since operators spend more time with their machines than anyone else. If they are well informed about basic machine operation, they will be able to detect the initial symptoms of machine trouble. Operators should also work with maintenance crews in detecting problems, determining their cause, and taking action to eliminate them.

Exhibit 8.6. Initial Symptoms of Machine Trouble

This approach may still seem difficult to digest for some people. However, in a way it can be compared to caring for our cars. If we are planning to drive a car across the desert, we will be quite careful about noise, vibration, or leaks. Additionally we may consider preparing a tool kit, and acquiring a basic understanding of maintenance work before we actually set out. We may wash the car by hand instead of using an automated car wash so that we can inspect it at the same time. If we find cracks or wear on the tires, or scratches on the body, we will have a better chance of avoiding big problems later on. If we listen carefully, we will also be able to detect the difference in the sound of the car's engine on rainy days as compared to dry sunny days.

Preventive measures are also important in caring for our bodies, as well as our cars and machines, and these are compared in Exhibit 8.7.

If there are people who still think that operators do not need to

Exhibit 8.7 A Comparison of Preventive Measures

	Body	Car	Machine
Problem:	Sickness	Breakdown	Breakdown
Cause of Problem	Lack of physical strength	Lack of maintenance	Lack of maintenance/lack of machine knowledge
Professional help	Doctor	Mechanic	Maintenance crews
Preventive care	Proper rest and exercise	Driving normally	Follow operating standards
Early detection of problems	Weight check	Oil check, hand wash	Noise, heat, vibration, etc.

know about machines but only how to produce products, that is a big mistake. In order for machines to perform at 100 percent of their capability, operators should be educated to detect abnormal conditions. They need to understand basic machine structure, function, adjustment methods, appropriate operational procedures, daily checkpoints, and so on.

A daily inspection is one of the first steps to familiarize operators with the machines. In these inspections, operators can use their five senses.

Obviously, we need to define ways to measure the degree of machine deterioration, or to develop certain standards to take action to regain the original level. An example in Exhibit 8.8 shows an easy way to detect problems associated with bolt tightening. Clearly, it is important to apply the correct torque level when retightening the bolt in order to maintain the normal condition.

Exhibit 8.8. A Visual Aid for Bolt Tightening

Painted Line

- Correct torque level should be applied when tightening.
- Painted line will enable us to monitor the appropriateness of bolt position.

One point to note here is that by retightening tens of thousands of bolts, at one time, a Japanese company found that it eliminated 80 percent of the machine breakdowns in the factory.

Cleaning the Machines

While the operators' daily inspection is a key step toward better machine maintenance, cleaning the machines also ties to inspection activity and forms the foundation for *total productive maintenance* (TPM)—an activity of total employee involvement in achieving minimum waste through maintenance operations.

At the beginning, many operators may protest that maintenance is not their responsibility, or that it is a waste of time since machines will get dirty anyway, or that it is better to increase production than to spend time cleaning machines. But as cleaning routines are established, and operators develop the ability to detect abnormal conditions, they find it more rewarding to take good care of the machines.

Since cleaning means touching different parts of the machine, as in the case of hand car washing described above, this work can be combined with inspection. It cannot be emphasized enough that cleaning and inspection are the most important activities in finding abnormal conditions in machines. With the help of maintenance crews, operators can learn to find abnormal conditions.

Four Phases of Machine Maintenance

In the preceding discussions, we have addressed the process of solving problems as they surface. We have emphasized the need to face problems on the shop floor and question the cause of the problems by asking "why" five times. This way we can eliminate recurring problems. We have also described the process of preventing machine-related troubles by addressing the need for active operator involvement in inspection, machine cleaning, bolt tightening, and so on. The improvement process will be a combination of these efforts. The following approach will help us eliminate machine-failure problems in a step-by-step fashion.

In the first of the four phases of machine maintenance (see Exhibit 8.9), forced deterioration is taking place because people are not taking responsibility for routine maintenance such as oiling and bolt

Exhibit 8.9. A Four-Phased Approach to Machine Failure Problems

Note: This approach was originally described in *TPM Evolution Program,* edited by Seiichi Nakajima (published by Japan Institute of Plant Maintenance, Japan, 1982).

tightening. This has to be changed. Also, restoration work needs to be done to regain the original level of machine performance. Obviously, cleaning the machines is the prerequisite for any maintenance activities.

In the second phase, where only natural deterioration of machines takes place, periodic preventive maintenance work starts to pay back. Machines are operated under prescribed conditions together with efforts in cleaning, inspecting, bolt tightening, and the like.

In the third phase, efforts to restore machines to their operating condition take place on a continuous basis. Operators are involved in identifying abnormal conditions to prevent machine deterioration. They use their five senses along with knowledge gained from maintenance crews. Operators are also able to repair many abnormal conditions by themselves.

The skills of the operators and maintenance crews are increased to avoid mistakes which may cause misoperations. Also, poka-yoke (foolproof mechanisms) and other improvement ideas are incorporated to prevent these misoperations. In addition to this, certain machine parts may be redesigned to extend machine life.

In the fourth phase, condition-based maintenance takes place— that is, the machine's condition is monitored constantly so that timely maintenance work can be done. With the use of diagnostic equipment, machine parts life and quality level of a processed workpiece can be forecasted and maintenance costs thereby reduced. Diagnostic equipment may include vibration monitors, shock pulse meters, and ultrasonic meters, which are most effective when the following conditions are met: First, machines are monitored regularly by operators looking for signs of deterioration. With such efforts, the proper use of certain types of diagnostic equipment and parameters of measurement becomes apparent. Without such efforts, most advanced diagnostic equipment may not suit the purpose or may become less cost effective. Second, machines need to be operated under prescribed conditions. If this is not done, diagnostic equipment may be monitoring very unreliable information or machine life may be too short for diagnostic equipment to be cost effective.

In short, the use of diagnostic equipment is like the use of robots or any other sophisticated equipment. Without understanding the functions and utilizing people's capabilities to evaluate alternative methods, the cost effectiveness of such equipment will be greatly reduced.

In the preceding part of this chapter, we addressed the fundamental approaches to improving machine maintenance. One of the key points to remember is that it takes everybody's coordination to make significant improvements. Operators, supervisors, maintenance crews, engineers, quality control people, and all other employees need to be a part of this process of improvement. Expanding on these points, the rest of this chapter will address the concept of total productive maintenance.

TOTAL PRODUCTIVE MAINTENANCE

Total productive maintenance (TPM) is a concept that involves all employees. The goal of TPM is to achieve overall effectiveness of the production system through employee participation in productive maintenance activities. The emphasis in TPM is on respect for the individual. In this sense, TPM is similar to total quality control (TQC), where involvement of employees is a key to success in developing quality operation of the business to meet customer needs. The development process of TPM is also similar to that of TQC. For example, machine breakdown or failure may be compared to product defects. Just as quality is to be built into the process rather than achieved through inspections, productive maintenance is much more desirable than breakdown maintenance. (See Exhibit 8.10 for a comparison of TPM and TQC.)

Exhibit 8.10. A Comparison of TPM and TQC

	TPM	TQC
Problem:	Machine breakdown	Product defects
Traditional solution:	Breakdown maintenance/ replacement of broken machine parts	End-of-line inspection/ sorting and rework
Improved solution:	Condition-based maintenance	In-process inspection
	Preventive maintenance	Poka-yoke (foolproof mechanism)
	Maintenance prevention	Design for quality
Information for monitoring:	Machine trouble record/ MTBF (mean time between failure)	Statistical process control/ control chart
Basic approaches:	Education	Education
	Employee involvement "Maintenance is free"	Employee involvement "Quality is free"

TPM Activities to Prevent Machine Failures

Machine failure is associated with the way people think and behave. Unless these processes are changed, there will continue to be machine breakdowns. In order to eliminate this, operators, maintenance crews, and other support people should understand how their roles interact and what they must do to support one another.

An effective approach to achieving zero failures is to eliminate the *potential* causes of failure, such as dust, rattles, loosened bolts, scratches, deformities, and wear. Failure is often the result of a combination of these factors, and unless these are addressed, the pursuit of eliminating failures will be fruitless.

When production people are asked by maintenance crews to stop production for machine maintenance, a negative response is most often observed. However, even during the busy production schedule, we should insist on stopping production for maintenance. An hour spent on maintenance will save tens of hours of shutdown time caused by machine failure.

Production people should be trained to help achieve zero production failures as follows: They should (1) learn how to do routine housekeeping, oiling, bolt tightening, etc., to prevent forced deterioration of machines; (2) receive instruction in proper operating procedures; and (3) develop an enhanced awareness of signs of early machine deterioration by performing easy maintenance, daily checks, setups, and so on.

The role of maintenance people, on the other hand, is to: (1) help the production people with self-maintenance activities, (2) restore deteriorating equipment through inspection, disassembly, and readjustment, (3) determine weaknesses in machine designs, take corrective actions, and specify operating conditions, and (4) help operators increase maintenance skills.

Summary

Zero machine troubles can be achieved more effectively by involving operators in maintaining normal machine operating conditions, detecting abnormal machine conditions as early as possible, and developing countermeasures to regain normal machine conditions.

This requires development of a close working relationship among operators, maintenance crews, and other support people as well as skill development and training to increase the abilities of those involved.

The use of advanced diagnostic systems and computerized maintenance scheduling generally becomes most effective after involvement of operators is developed. Otherwise, we may be simply automating the inefficiencies.

Chapter 9

Scheduling a Steady Flow for Better Control

When things are constantly changing, they are difficult to control. As the principles of quality control emphasize eliminating scatter, so we need to think of ways to reduce the level of fluctuation in all areas of our manufacturing activity. In principle, this can be done by standardizing operations. In this chapter and the next, therefore, we will discuss (1) the approaches to developing a steady flow of material throughout the factory, and (2) the basic elements of standardized operations.

In this chapter, leveling the production schedule for a given period will be described as an important approach to developing steady material flow. With this in place, each person engaged in production will be able to control his or her area with certain expectations. This will contribute to establishing a more manageable situation and will make improvement activities much easier.

LEVELED/MIXED PRODUCTION

Turning to the final assembly line where the finished goods come out, we still find that many such lines all over the world operate in a fashion similar to batch processing machines. The same kind of product may be produced for a day, a week, or even longer before the next product comes out.

This is similar to the situation we discussed in Chapter 3, of long setups associated with large production batch sizes. Frequent changeovers are generally unpopular because they interrupt the steady flow of work. However, just as we have discussed the need for setup time reduction, we should work on reducing the setup time required for the assembly line as well.

As Exhibit 9.1 suggests, when different products are produced in a mixed fashion every day or every hour or even every minute, the finished goods inventory level will be significantly lower. (We call this mode of production *mixed production*.) Also, fine tuning of the mix will make it easier to reduce the risk of overproducing any one product.

At one time manufacturers could offer customers a single product of a standardized size and shape, but with increased world competition and diversified user needs, a manufacturer's ability to respond quickly to the market can become an issue of survival.

We should also note that end users, as a group, typically consume products in certain patterns, except during certain promotional periods. As mixed production closely reflects the market demand profile, it transmits this demand profile to subassembly and fabrication areas more accurately than the batch production mode. Under the mixed production mode, varieties of parts are consumed at a fairly steady rate. This enables upstream operations to control production more readily than before.

Exhibit 9.1. Benefits of Mixed Production

125

This steadiness is very important in managing factories and addressing improvement activities. We can easily imagine the effect of sudden changes in production schedules if such steadiness is lacking.

While mixed production will make the total production operation smoother, the sudden production volume change will have a negative effect if it is not managed well. This is why *leveling* the total production volume becomes important.

By leveling the schedule, as depicted in Exhibit 9.2, production people can focus their attention on production activities without having to worry much about sudden schedule changes or expediting work. Together with mixed production, quick setups, and flow production concepts, leveled scheduling can vastly improve line performance and reduce parts shortage problems.

Exhibit 9.2. A Leveled Production Schedule Can Help Cope with Fluctuating Market Demand

Market Demand Profile Leveled Production Schedule

Even if we understand the benefits of *leveled/mixed production* and monthly production volume is set, actual production levels may still vary in a fashion known as end-of-month crisis pattern (see Exhibit 9.3a). In this pattern, parts are produced early in the month and stored as in-process inventory. Towards the end of the month, everybody may be struggling to meet the monthly production goal. The assembly line will be at its busiest, together with some lines that must produce missing parts.

Clearly, in a leveled/mixed production scheme, this should not be allowed. One approach to leveled/mixed production, therefore, is first to divide a month into two periods (two-week "time buckets"; see Exhibit 9.3b) and then to reduce the lot size and practice frequent changeovers in the final assembly line as well as in other lines to meet the biweekly goals.

When this is accomplished, we can then cut each time bucket in half (i.e., two one-week time buckets; Exhibit 9.3c), and proceed in

Exhibit 9.3. An Approach to Establishing Production Linearity

—— Actual production profile — — — Leveled schedule profile

a similar fashion until total production linearity is established (Exhibit 9.3d).

In order to make leveled production work, both sales and production people need to decide on the fixed level of production volume and its duration. Whether a company is marketing driven or manufacturing driven, both sides need to understand each other very well in order to arrive at the best solution for the company. At the same time, both sides need to do their best to help each other. For example, production might improve flexibility and lead time, while sales and marketing could improve the accuracy of their forecast and reduce the information lead time for order-taking.

As you see in Exhibit 9.4, similar problems exist in the office and factory environment. It is especially important that top management and those who coordinate production and sales activities understand this in order to gain maximum benefits for the company.

Exhibit 9.4. Typical Problems Observed in Our Offices and Factories

Offices	Factories
Long information lead time	Long production lead time
Large information lot size	Large production lot size
Large information inventory	Large inventory

Note: By exchanging the terms "factory" for "office," "machine" for "copier" or "computer terminal," "workpiece" for "paper," and "warehouse" for "file cabinet," we find that the same principles described in this book equally apply to order taking, invoicing, and other information-processing activities.

In the factory environment, the benefits from leveled/mixed production are significant. It will result in a smooth flow of parts and even workloads throughout the factory. Unnecessary expediting, checking, rework, and delays are minimized, as are the finished product and work-in-process (WIP) inventories. By producing the products with a similar mix and a fixed volume for a certain time period, scheduling becomes easier, and operators can concentrate on their work. Of course, short setup times, small lot production, and associated changes are necessary to make this possible.

With a standardized level schedule developed for a week to a month depending on the nature of the market and the capability of the factory, problems become easy to identify for improvement and such improvement becomes visible to everyone in the factory when implemented.

As Exhibit 9.5 shows, leveled/mixed production provides a means for us to make the production people's work easier. While a certain amount of finished goods inventory may be necessary, focusing on WIP inventory reduction through leveled/mixed production generally pays off much more than just focusing on reducing the finished goods inventory. This finished goods inventory will function as a breakwater to protect upstream processes from the fluctuation of demand. (Please note, however, that for certain manufacturers, the location of the breakwater may be shifted to upstream processes as appropriate.)

We should also remember the improvement potential in production lead time as lot size is reduced and other wastes, such as transportation, are minimized. A factor of ten or more in reduction of production lead time will make the sales and marketing people's jobs easier, reducing the need for an accurate forecast.

With these changes, many make-to-stock companies have successfully converted their operations to make-to-order.

Exhibit 9.5. Finished Goods Inventory Helps Smooth Production Activities

Examples

- Exhibit 9.6 shows an example of mixed production in a Japanese refrigerator factory where large- and small-sized refrigerators are produced in a mixed production mode.
- When producing many different kinds of products on one line, it becomes necessary to determine the sequence so that certain operational priorities can be considered in setting up schedules. This process may be done by using a computer to determine the optimum pattern considering many different operational preferences.
- When different kinds of products are produced on the same line, and some are found to be more time consuming than others, careful planning is required to avoid confusion. A typical solution is (1) to pair the most time-consuming product with the least time-consuming product, or (2) to change the work procedures so that each operator's work content remains balanced. Of course, improvement efforts should be made to re-

Exhibit 9.6. Mixed Production of Different Sizes of Refrigerators

duce the work content of the most time-consuming product. But when the difference in work content is still very large, a bypass method should be used (see Exhibit 9.7).

Exhibit 9.7. Use of a Bypass Line for Time-Consuming Products

Net Working Time
A : 15 min
B : 16 min
C : 18 min
D : 25 min

When there is a change in production mix, further adjustments become necessary. Also, it should be noted that the production sequence may be changed after the bypass line. The line should be able to accommodate these situations.

CYCLE TIME CONTROL

When leveled/mixed production is established, we can expect final assembly to complete a product at a certain interval, such as 1 minute

per unit or 1 hour per unit. This becomes a rhythm, driving operations throughout the factory. Just as a river flows at a certain speed to the ocean, all operations will be balanced based upon this interval, or *cycle time,* as it is called here. Sometimes, production lead time is also called cycle time, but we do not use it here in such a way. (See Exhibit 9.8.)

Exhibit 9.8. Definition of Cycle Time and Production Lead Time

Cycle time: Time between the completion of the last product and completion of the next product

Production lead time: Time between beginning of production and completion of production

$$\text{Cycle time} = \frac{\text{Available production time in a day}}{\text{Required production units in a day}}$$

While cycle time may be determined from the available time for production and required production volume, it should not be considered as fixed. Any operation should be able to accommodate the changes requested by the next process within a certain predetermined range. For example, a machine problem should stop the line so that the problem area is exposed. We should remember that the next process is your customer and that only the products requested by the customer should be produced.

The following example will explain the benefits of cycle time control.

Example: Assembly Line

By rearranging work and making a dozen small improvements to the assembly line, the number of operators is reduced from six to five (Exhibit 9.9). Note how the improvements expose operator E's unutilized time. This becomes a target for further improvement in the future. If operator E's unutilized time is spread out among all op-

Exhibit 9.9. Cycle Time Concept Helps Work Allocation Among Operators

erators, on the other hand, the problem is hidden and difficult to improve further (see Exhibit 9.10).

When we eliminate a position by improvement, it is best to move the most skillful operator away to another position (e.g., an improvement team) so that the rest of the operators do not feel concerned with job security. At the same time, we can create opportunity for them to expand their skills for advancement.

Example: Fabrication Shop

The approach is the same in a fabrication shop as in an assembly line. Exhibit 9.11 shows the change in staffing a machining line following a change in the cycle time. Five machines are arranged in a U-shaped form and the work is done by one-piece production.

This example shows production flexibility. When planning the machine layout, consideration should be given to keeping the work combinations flexible, so that it becomes easy to rearrange work according to the production volume.

Exhibit 9.10. Comparison of Work Allocation Among Operators

Good example of
work allocation:

- Unutilized time is
 easy to see

- High incentive to
 improve further

Bad example of
work allocation:

- Unutilized time
 is hidden

- No incentive to
 improve further

Exhibit 9.11. Cycle Time and Staffing Requirements in a U-Shaped
Line

Note: Multifunctional operators help cope with the change in
market demand and establish standardized work accordingly.

133

SUMMARY

It can be difficult to cope with the constant changes that accompany fluctuating product variety and volume. One solution is mixed production, where different products are produced in a mixed fashion. This results in lower finished goods inventories, shorter production lead time, and easier fine tuning of production to product mix changes.

Leveled production keeps production volume constant for a certain period of time. This will result in less confusion on the shop floor. It is also easier to expose and deal with problems.

Using the cycle time control concept will keep the production cycle between products constant to follow the leveled production concept. With this, operator's underutilized time will be easily exposed to facilitate further improvement.

When these concepts are practiced together with other improvement techniques discussed earlier, production activity becomes much more streamlined and improvement activities take place much more easily. In practicing these concepts, however, we need to carefully establish and use standards as explained further in the next chapter.

Improving with Standards

Without standards, improvement potential is very much limited. Things will fall back to a chaotic state and there may be only fire-fighting work left for us to do.

First, we must set standards and practice the concept of "management by exception." For each exception to a given set of standards, we need first to solve the problem and then to improve the standard so that the same problem does not recur.

With more standards in place, we can do more jobs with less confusion. At the same time, people can pick up new jobs without much difficulty. These points are especially important in producing high quality goods by people who may be rotating their jobs or handling more functions than before.

Once standards have been established, they must be constantly monitored and revised quickly when necessary, to reflect improvement activities including operators' suggestions.

STANDARD WORK

As production is leveled and cycle time established, we start to see a discipline established throughout the factory. In fact, operating a factory may be compared to playing music in an orchestra. As there are three basic elements in music, so factory operation also requires three similar elements (see Exhibit 10.1).

Exhibit 10.1. Three Elements of Music and Factory Operation

Music	Factory Operation
Rhythm:	Cycle time
Tone:	Quality operation of each work center
Harmony:	Line balance

As *rhythm* in music drives the whole orchestra to synchronize with the swing of the conductor's baton, cycle time in a factory will drive the production line with a smooth, steady flow of goods. In fact, the Japanese also refer to cycle time as "tact" time, reflecting the rhythmical swing of the baton.

Tone is, as distinguished from noise, a beautiful sound coming out of such instruments as the violin or flute. This is compared to machines producing good-quality products. Only through practicing good maintenance and quality at the source can a factory produce the desired output.

Harmony, then, is the coordination of individually different sounds. Just as an orchestra cannot perform well if each individual player is concerned only with his or her performance, the coordination of different operations, or line balance, in a factory is a key to well-integrated performance.

Only when these elements are in place can an orchestra play beautiful music.

Standard work in the factory is similar to the music score for each musician. In our factories, standard work is a tool to achieve maximum performance with minimum waste.

As market demands change, however, our factories also need to change. Therefore, standard work needs to be revised. New machines, new tools, or new methods may be introduced periodically, making it necessary to modify and update standard work practices.

If practices are not updated periodically, no real improvement has taken place. Exhibit 10.2 shows the cycle of improvement reflecting this point.

This cycle may proceed in the following fashion:

1. Study the current operation and standardize work procedures
2. Find the problem areas
3. Solve problems and develop improved methods

Exhibit 10.2. Cycle of Improvement

4. Implement new methods
5. If new methods are satisfactory, develop new standard work and continue the cycle from item 2.

In a just-in-time production environment, this standard work should be composed of three elements: cycle time, work sequence, and standard amount of work-in-process (see Exhibit 10.3).

Exhibit 10.3. The Three Elements of Standard Work

Cycle time:	Time between the completion of the last product and completion of the next product
Work sequence:	Workers' sequence of work (not necessarily the same as the sequence of material flow)
Standard amount of work-in-process:	Minimum amount of WIP inventory necessary to conduct smooth operation (this includes parts for machines)

Standard work is not just something that staff or supervisors demand the operators to comply with. The whole idea is to involve operators as well as supervisors in the development process. The standard work should be developed in such a manner that anyone can follow the instructions. Ideally, beginners should be able to master the standard work within three days of training. In order to achieve this, it is important to improve and simplify the work process, as well as to have trainers to help the beginners.

A *standard work sheet* may be displayed at each work center enabling anyone to follow the instructions (see Exhibit 10.4). It also serves the purpose of helping supervisors review whether the work was conducted as prescribed. By noting the revision date on the standard work sheet, we would also know how actively improvement activities have taken place. A standard work sheet is, therefore, not

just a tool for instructing people, but also a tool for further improvement.

WORK COMBINATION CHART

Work combination charts are used to allocate operators' areas of responsibility and to develop standard work based on cycle time. Exhibit 10.4 shows the machining operation of an automotive parts manufacturer in the Midwest. Exhibits 10.5 and 10.6 are examples of work combination charts. The chart in Exhibit 10.5 was developed by a manufacturing engineer in a midwestern company using a personal computer. Machining time and operators' work procedures can be easily explained to both engineers and operators, assuring that there is no conflict between operator and machine in the work procedures.

Exhibit 10.6 is a chart used at Toyota and its affiliates. The principle is the same as that for Exhibit 10.5. The difference is that the first chart depends on *standard time* as calculated by engineers whereas Toyota emphasizes using the actual time as measured on the spot.

Example: Electronic Products Manufacturer

Exhibit 10.7 shows the assembly operation of a Silicon Valley electronic products manufacturer.

In this example, the entire line operations were analyzed by using the work combination charts. Cycle time was established by selecting a certain conveyor speed. The standard quantity of work-in-process inventory was determined by placing each work unit between the pitch marks. (Pitch marks were drawn on the conveyor at specified intervals corresponding to the cycle time.) The work sequence was written on the display, which was located at each work station, and a line stop button was provided for each operator.

In order to monitor each operator's progress, work element lines may be drawn on the conveyor frame. With these lines, an operator will know how he is progressing within the cycle time.

The results of the time and motion study as explained on a work

Exhibit 10.4. Example of Standard Work Sheet

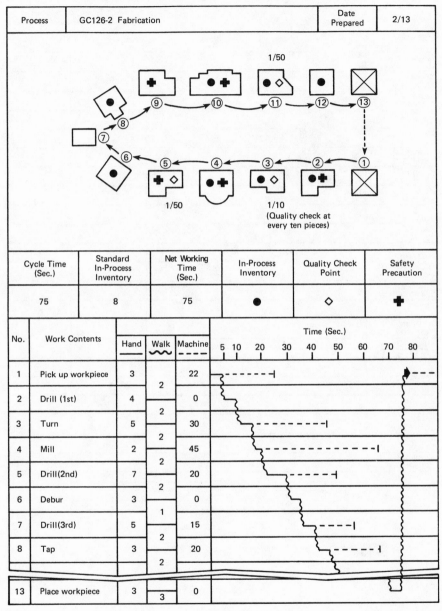

| Process | GC126-2 Fabrication | | | | Date Prepared | 2/13 |

Cycle Time (Sec.)	Standard In-Process Inventory	Net Working Time (Sec.)	In-Process Inventory	Quality Check Point	Safety Precaution
75	8	75	●	◇	✚

No.	Work Contents	Hand	Walk ∿	Machine ---	Time (Sec.) 5 10 20 30 40 50 60 70 80
1	Pick up workpiece	3	2	22	
2	Drill (1st)	4	2	0	
3	Turn	5	2	30	
4	Mill	2	2	45	
5	Drill(2nd)	7	2	20	
6	Debur	3	1	0	
7	Drill(3rd)	5	2	15	
8	Tap	3	2	20	
13	Place workpiece	3	3	0	

1/50

1/50 1/10
(Quality check at
every ten pieces)

139

Exhibit 10.5. Example of Work Combination Chart

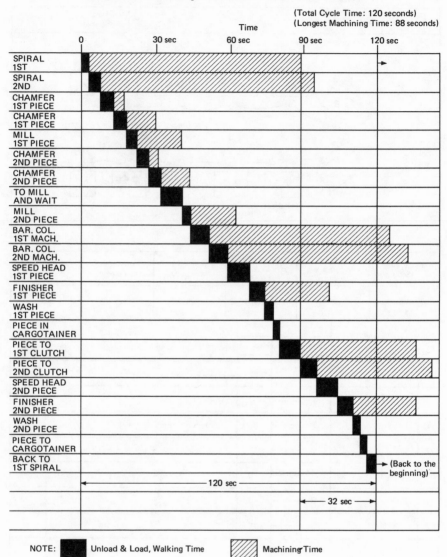

Exhibit 10.6. Standard Work Combination Chart

No.	Content of Work	Time			Time
		Hand	Machine	Walk	5″ 10″ 15″ 20″25″30″35″ 40″ 45″ 50″ 55″60″65″ 70″ 75″80″ 85″

Part No. | Process Name | Standard Work Combination Chart | Date | Section | Daily Volume | Cycle Time | — Hand Work ····· Machine Work ⟋⟍⟋⟍Walk

Net Work Time (Hand work time + walk time)

Exhibit 10.7. Use of Pitch Marks to Help Practice Standard Work

141

combination chart are shown in Exhibit 10.8. In this exhibit, station 3 is shown as an example. Exhibit 10.9 shows the work combination charts for six of the stations according to the flow of material. These results are then summarized in Exhibit 10.10 to show the work contents of each station.

Exhibit 10.8. Work Combination Chart for Station 3

The process of analysis, summary of the findings, and the process of generating improvement ideas are briefly listed below:

Process of Analysis.

1. Observe processes
2. Fill out work combination charts for all stations
3. Determine the cycle time
4. Rebalance line to fully utilize operators' time

Major Findings.

1. Station 5 has the highest work content, while station 1 (work preparation and inspection) has the lowest.
2. Handling time is extensive, i.e., 34 percent of total operating time.
3. Utilization of total operators' time is 74 percent of total available time.

Exhibit 10.9. Use of Work Combination Chart at a Computer Manufacturer

Exhibit 10.10. Analysis of Work Content by Work Station

Total handling time = 318 sec. (34%)

Total net working time = 611 sec (66%)

Total operating time = 929 sec. (100%)

$$\text{Utilization of operator's time} = \frac{\text{Total operating time}}{\text{Cycle time} \times \text{Number of operators}}$$

$$= \frac{929}{126 \times 10} = 74\%$$

Generating Improvement Ideas.

1. Move operations where feasible in order to fully utilize operators' time at all work stations. Present utilization indicates that the whole operation can be done by fewer than eight operators.
2. Study material handling, practice workplace organization, develop or improve fixtures, and use devices such as gravity-fed racks in order to reduce operators' handling time.
3. Reduce the distance between operators, perform operations in a standing position where possible, and develop relay zone arrangement so that neighboring operators can easily help each other.

SUMMARY

In this chapter, we have reviewed the importance of standardized work practices in the manufacturing environment. One of the points emphasized was the orientation toward improvement rather than simply instituting rigid standards. Also, since operator involvement is so important in achieving efficient operations, we need to develop standards that they can practice easily.

Several examples were included to illustrate the usage of standards in improvement activities. While the use of time and motion study techniques to effect improvements is rare in most American manufacturing industries, the potential impact of these practices deserves greater attention. A Japanese automobile company, for example, used this basic technique for its sophisticated body-welding operations conducted by robots and succeeded in reducing the number of robots from twenty-four to nineteen.

Often, a company's competitive advantage results from the degree to which each participant pays attention to improvement activities and practicing standards. In this sense, it should be noted that Toyota practices improvement activities to reduce operator work time by as little as half a second. Each improvement idea may be viewed as common sense, but there is a big difference between practicing it and not practicing it. Also, there is a big difference between idea generation and recommendations prepared solely by staff engineers and those done by involving line people.

Chapter 11

Tying Things Together

In the first ten chapters, we have discussed such subjects as good housekeeping and workplace organization, quick setup, developing a physical flow of materials, flexible operators, visual control and jidoka (autonomation) concepts, productive maintenance, leveled/mixed production, and standardized work. In order to produce goods in the required amount at the required time, at the lowest cost and at highest quality, however, we need to control and coordinate these different activities. This involves developing a just-in-time information and control system where all necessary information arrives on time at the place where action is to be taken.

In order to achieve this, kanban, the broadcast system, and other communication techniques are discussed in this chapter. Furthermore, we will see that these tools do not merely serve the function of providing information on time. They are also used to facilitate further improvement.

KANBAN

Just-in-time production means producing required parts, at the required time, in the required amount, at each step of the production process in the most economical manner. Smooth flow of materials throughout our own factories, as well as in our suppliers' factories, is of course the ideal.

Reduced setup times, product-oriented layouts, one-piece flow production arrangements with multiprocess handling, and lev-

eled/mixed production help to develop such a flow. But when there is a physical distance between processes or there is a long lead time in the upstream processes, we need to think of a way to tie the processes together. These processes need to function as if they were connected by invisible conveyors.

Kanban, which means "display card" in Japanese, is one such production control tool. It is also a tool to facilitate improvement, as will be explained later. Unfortunately, however, there has been some misunderstanding of its usage and purpose. Some people equate just-in-time (JIT) production to kanban, or equate kanban to an inventory control system. These are fallacies. In order for us to benefit fully, we must fully understand the role of kanban and its relationship to the rest of the production activities.

We will see that kanban only functions effectively in combination with other elements of JIT, such as leveled/mixed production schedule, good workplace organization, and flow production. When these elements are combined, the power of a new production system will be realized.

American Supermarkets and Kanban

To understand the fundamentals of the kanban concept, the story of Toyota's Mr. Taiichi Ohno, founder of the just-in-time production system, is helpful.*

Mr. Ohno had already heard of the efficiency of the American supermarket system before he visited the United States for the first time in 1956. He was most interested in understanding the supermarket method and its applications in the production arena. Mr. Ohno saw that the supermarket could be equated with the upstream process in a factory. The downstream process (customer) goes to the upstream process (supermarket) to obtain the required parts (commodities) at the required time in the required amount. The upstream process then makes up the amount of goods for the next process (customer) to pick up again later.

Mr. Ohno had begun to introduce this supermarket method in Toyota's machining factory in 1953 before his visit to the United States. He confirmed his idea that just-in-time production was possible during his visit. Among the many problems he faced in devel-

*Taiichi Ohno, *Toyota Production System,* Diamond Publishing Company, 1978.

Exhibit 11.1. A Scene at a Supermarket

oping a new production system, however, was the confusion of setting up the priority of work at the upstream process. Problems were created because the downstream process would carry away a large amount of a certain part at one time. After much trial and error, the solution reached was leveled/mixed production scheduling. Without this, the supermarket system could not function well. In theory, of course the system will work if there is a huge amount of inventory. Practically, it was not feasible.

What Is Kanban?

Kanban is a tool introduced to make this supermarket system work. Kanban is a Japanese word meaning "display" or "instruction card." In a factory setting, it is a card describing the part number, the quantity of parts, where they are from, to where they are to be delivered, and so on. With this as a base, let us first examine how kanban cards would function if we applied them in the supermarket setting.

When customers pick up goods from the shelf, the goods will have kanban cards attached to them. At the checkout, when the customers pay the bill, all kanban cards are collected so that the store people will know how many goods have been sold during a certain period. Collected cards are then sent to the purchasing department where purchasing agents will "pull" from the warehouse the same amount of goods as described on the cards collected.

If we imagine that there is a factory attached to the warehouse, we may have "production" cards attached to goods stored in the warehouse. The kanban cards collected by purchasing agents (we will call them "move" cards) will be exchanged with "production" cards before goods are withdrawn.

Now, we have production cards equal to the amount of goods sold. When these cards are collected by production people in the factory, the corresponding goods will be manufactured in the amount requested by the production cards. The goods are then transferred to the warehouse with production cards attached to them.

With this "supermarket" method of material handling and production activities the whole function of scheduling and expediting may be reduced, and material flow and production will be controlled by each of those people involved in handling cards. Therefore, the roles of scheduling and expediting people may change to simply monitoring or updating the system.

Exhibit 11.2 illustrates the sequence of events as follows.

1. A customer picks up the goods he wants from the shelf.
2. At the checkout, move cards are removed from goods and put into a box (kanban post).
3. Move cards are sent to the warehouse. As goods are picked up to refill the shelf, move cards are exchanged for the production cards that were attached to the goods.

Exhibit 11.2. The Supermarket Concept and Use of Kanban

Note: ╱ : move card
 ⌀ : production card

4. As the exchange takes place, production cards are collected in the box (another kanban post)
5. The goods picked up are brought back to the supermarket shelves with move cards attached to them.
6. Production cards are brought back to the factory, where operators will manufacture only the amount indicated by the production cards.
7. When production is completed, production cards are attached to those goods manufactured.
8. Goods are transferred to the warehouse. End of cycle.

This example might illustrate what Mr. Ohno of Toyota had in mind in the 1950s. But some questions may arise:

Q: Can we use electronic data processing, such as the use of bar codes and optical code readers for transfer or collection of certain information?

A: Yes, these are used in some factories, especially when a great many products are involved and certain monitoring is necessary, e.g., for accounts payable to suppliers, etc.

Q: How do we determine the number of cards?

A: We will not answer this question in detail here, but the number will depend on production volume, volume fluctuation, lead time to refill, container size, etc. Different numbers can be tried out and modified as necessary.

Q: Is it not creating a waste of double handling to have a warehouse between factory and supermarket?

A: Yes, it is much better if we can eliminate the warehouse and transfer goods directly from the factory. Depending on production lead time, nature of customer demand, distance between the factory and supermarket, etc., this may or may not be feasible.

Q: What happens if we eliminate the warehouse?

A: There will be only one kind of card instead of both move and production cards. This card should be collected at the checkout and sent back to the factory, where it is attached to the goods produced. Goods with cards will then be brought directly back to the corresponding shelves. This may be called a one-card system as opposed to the two-card system we described before.

Q: Is it okay to have one card for a group of goods?

A: Yes, but we should make sure that each group can be easily identified, e.g., by using standard containers for a certain number of goods. Of course, the containers may be made returnable.

Q: If containers are designated by color or some other means, do we still need cards? Can containers function as cards by themselves?

A: Yes, that is possible, and often done where there is less confusion in doing so.

Q: How do we compare this supermarket example with actual factory operations?

A: Exhibit 11.3 may explain what can happen in a factory setting.

Q: The exhibit shows lots of storage areas. Aren't these considered wasteful?

Exhibit 11.3. Kanban Routes in a Factory

Note: P : Production Card
M : Move Card

151

A: Yes, we do not want these storage areas or the inventories and waste associated with them. Therefore, we should always try to be creative in eliminating this waste. To do so, we can, for example, tie the parts fabrication line to the assembly line where applicable. We should also remember that we can be innovative in using the kanban concept in a variety of ways to fit each situation.

Functions of Kanban

In order to implement kanban effectively, we need to understand its two functions clearly. One is production control; the other is process improvement.

The production control function is to tie different processes together and to develop a just-in-time system so that required materials will arrive at the required time in the required amount throughout the factory, even including suppliers' factories whenever possible.

The process improvement function is to facilitate improvement activities in the factory through the use of kanban. This is done by using the approaches described in earlier chapters of this book. With an emphasis on reducing the inventory levels through a reduction in the number of kanban cards, the whole improvement activity will be enhanced.

In the following section, we will address these two functions in more detail. Let us review first the necessary considerations before introducing kanban, so that we will not fall into serious problems later on.

Homework Before Introducing Kanban

Just as Taiichi Ohno struggled to introduce kanban in the 1950s, many of us may encounter difficulties if we are not well prepared. Certain struggles may be beneficial for deepening our insight, but they may also be costly if we do not handle the situation well. In that sense, we should realize that there are also failures associated with the introduction of kanban. For example, because of a lack of understanding, one Japanese company incurred years of losses before regaining its position after refining the kanban concept.

To avoid serious mistakes, we need to do some homework before introducing kanban. Even though the situations may differ by individual companies' production characteristics, the two items that

need to be addressed first are leveled/mixed production schedules and certain associated process improvements.

As discussed in Chapter 9, leveled/mixed scheduling helps us to develop a smooth flow in the factory. It also helps us to assess whether we have enough people, equipment, and materials ready to meet the schedule.

When kanban is introduced and a downstream process produces goods in a highly fluctuating fashion, or if customers purchase goods in large lots, all the upstream processes need to have enough extra capacity to absorb this fluctuation by adding more resources—that is, people and machines. We cannot allow this to happen if we are to be competitive. On the other hand, if an upstream process has only a small capacity, it will need to produce goods in advance. We cannot allow this to happen with kanban either, since kanban will be a tool for producing only the required goods, only when they are required, and only in the amount required at the time by the downstream process rather than producing goods in advance of demand.

Another important point to be addressed in connection with kanban is the whip effect or swing effect of production dynamics. As shown in Exhibit 11.4, changes in the final assembly schedule often result in a big swing toward the upstream processes. This occurs because of large lot production, a lack or delay of communication, quality problems, machine problems, and the like. Generally speaking, the further upstream we are, the greater the swing effect we tend to get.

With sudden changes in schedule, kanban cards for certain parts may turn around very quickly at one point in time, and very slowly at another. As a result, the handling of kanban may become difficult, and we may even end up with having more inventory or more parts shortages than before implementing kanban.

Exhibit 11.4. Propagation of "Wave" in the Factory

| Fabrication | Subassembly | Final Assembly |

Note: This concept was originally developed by Dr. Jay W. Forrester in "Industrial Dynamics," *Harvard Business Review* (July-August, 1958).

Also, with big swings in production, we may not be able to keep the flow of material in a certain predetermined routing, making the handling of kanban even more difficult. For these reasons we need to develop a leveled/mixed production schedule to smooth the existing material flow.

Leveled/mixed production should be practiced first at the final assembly line, but people there also need to understand its impact on all the people in upstream processes.

The more parts one pulls at a time, the bigger the impact on the upstream processes. The same situation applies to subassembly, fabrication, and suppliers' processes, all the way through the linkage of the production processes. The steadier the flow of materials with leveled/mixed production, the less disruption there will be in upstream processes.

Kanban functions, therefore, as a tool for fine tuning production while linking all of the processes as a chain. If there is a big fluctuation, kanban may not be able to function effectively. Rather, a chaotic situation may result.

Remember also that leveled/mixed production will help us to improve the processes. As discussed earlier, flow production processes should be developed so that at any point in time, there is a streamlined flow of material throughout the factory.

As discussed earlier, setup time reduction and small lot production are the prerequisites to practicing leveled/mixed schedule across the factory from final assembly to initial fabrication process. Also, one-piece flow production should be developed by modifying layouts and training multifunctional operators so that a smooth flow of material can be established as much as possible.

Furthermore, jidoka, visual control, poka-yoke, preventive maintenance, and other ideas need to be incorporated in order to eliminate potential disruptions to the system. Needless to say, top management's understanding and commitment are also a prerequisite.

After these preparations for the introduction of kanban have been made, there are still further specifics to be considered before actual implementation. These points are summarized as follows:

1. Sales/marketing people and production people need to get together and determine the production schedule for final assembly so that leveled/mixed production can be developed.
2. In developing a flow throughout the plant, a kanban route

should be established to reflect this flow. This requires designating locations so that there will be no confusion in material handling with kanban. The addressing of locations is a commonly used approach to this practice.

3. In order to develop a steady flow and practice leveled/mixed production throughout the plant, usage of kanban should be tied to small lot production and frequent changeover. Also, kanban cards should be attached to small containers, and circulated frequently so that production information will be transmitted to the upstream processes without much delay.

4. While kanban may be most suited to repetitive production items, certain infrequently ordered items, high value items, or bulky items may be treated differently, such as with the broadcast system (to be discussed later).

5. For seasonal and promotional items, and in the initial phase of new product introduction, where a large fluctuation or surge in production is expected, sales and marketing people should give sufficient prior notice to production people.

6. As the sales level changes, or as improvement activities take place, the whole kanban system needs to be updated. We need to review the number and content of kanban cards so that production activities can be conducted with a minimum level of inventory.

7. In order to use kanban, we need to develop a reliable rational production system. Kanban can help us do this, but ideally process improvement needs to be addressed first. Equipped with techniques for improvement, we should continue to improve the system by reducing the number of kanban cards. There is no end to improvement.

Rules of Kanban

Any tool has an appropriate method for using it. If we use it well, the tool will serve our purpose. But if we use it incorrectly, it can become an enemy. We can say the same thing with kanban. People involved in the kanban operation should understand and practice these fundamental rules (Exhibit 11.5).

The first rule represents the transportation order. In order to practice this with the kanban concept, the downstream process should

Exhibit 11.5. Rules of Kanban

1. People from a downstream process should obtain parts from the upstream process according to the information described on the detached kanban card (move card).
2. People in the production process should produce parts according to the information described on the kanban card (production card).
3. If there is no kanban card, there will be no production and no transfer of materials.
4. The kanban card should always be attached to the parts container unless it is in transit to order production or transportation of parts.
5. People in the production process should make sure that 100 percent quality parts are produced before putting them into the containers. If there is a defect, the line should stop to determine countermeasures.
6. The number of kanban cards should be gradually reduced in order to link processes better and expose waste for improvement.

follow the discipline of leveled/mixed production and transportation should be carried out at frequent intervals to help link the production processes tightly.

The second rule represents the production order. In order to meet this requirement, the upstream production process needs to be prepared so that any production order can be readily processed without delay. Production should be carried out according to the sequence of kanban cards received in order to maintain a steady flow and reduce the swing effect described earlier.

The third rule confirms the discipline of eliminating overproduction (and overtransportation) waste. When the first and second rules are practiced, this third rule should automatically follow.

When these rules are followed, production and transportation control is similar to the autonomic nervous and muscle systems in our bodies. Just as the functions of the heart and stomach can adjust to what we do (e.g., exercise, eating, sleeping), without direct intervention from the brain, production systems using kanban can function on their own without much involvement of the production control people.

The fourth rule corresponds to the idea of visual control. Kanban cards such as the one shown in Exhibit 11.6 can convey the key

Exhibit 11.6. Example of Kanban Used in Japan

operational information in a very handy way. The information may include production volume, method of production, and sequence for production cards or transportation volume, timing, locations (from and to), method of transportation, and container type for move cards. When this information is attached to containers, waste associated with overproduction can be avoided and information transfer becomes much simpler.

Since production and transportation information arrives at the appropriate time for people to take action as instructed by a kanban card, there is no unnecessary paperwork or information processing. The people's time associated with it is eliminated accordingly.

The fifth rule conveys the notion of the reflexive nerve and muscle systems in our bodies. When abnormal conditions arise, corrective action can be taken without the brain's involvement. Likewise, with the jidoka or line stop concept in place, abnormal conditions will be detected automatically, and we can keep our production system healthy by not passing a defective product to the downstream process. Exposing the problems of defective products may cause some embarrassment, but it prompts us to ask "why" several times and check into the cause of the problems.

The sixth rule is tied to the improvement enhancement function of kanban. As we have discussed in connection with the line stop concept, exposing problems will enhance the need for improvement. As the number of kanban cards is reduced in our pursuit of continuous improvement, and as inventory is correspondingly reduced, additional problems will become evident. We must then be constantly alert to new ideas for solving these problems.

Different Kinds of Kanban and Their Usages

Depending on the need, a variety of kanban are available. The major kinds of kanban are shown in Exhibit 11.7.

Exhibit 11.7. Types of Kanban

Production kanban are used for assembly lines and other areas where the setup time is virtually zero. For application on the conveyor line, the card should be placed in front of the first workpiece on the conveyor. When the cards cannot be attached to goods—for example, when heat treating is involved—they should be hung near the heat treatment process according to the sequence inside the process.

Exhibit 11.8. Types of Information on a Production Kanban Card

(Appearance)	Part No.	1 7 6 3 4 – 2 2 6 3 1 – 1 2		Process
	Name of Product	Piston Ring		Machining
	Container Type	S 10C	No. Issued	MC-12
	Container Capacity	200	2/5	

Signal kanban are used for lot production items in such areas as press, die casting, and injection moulding. By locating signal kanban at certain positions (such as reorder points) in parts storage areas, and specifying the production lot size, signal kanban will function just like production kanban. (See Exhibits 11.9 and 11.10.) While production kanban can be used instead of signal kanban by bundling them and starting production when a certain number of cards have

Exhibit 11.9. Machine, Signal Kanban, and Parts and Die Storage Areas

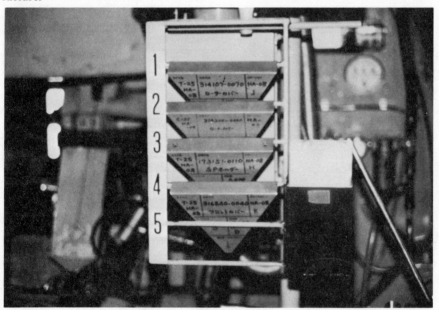

Exhibit 11.10. Example of Signal Kanban in a Japanese Automotive Parts Manufacturer

been collected, signal kanban are convenient to do minimum/maximum control for lot production items with one card.

In Exhibit 11.11, the signal kanban is detached when an operator starts to use the workpiece in the second container from the bottom. Production will start according to the sequence in which the signal kanban cards arrive at the machine.

In Exhibit 11.12, the material kanban is used to get the raw material. When both signal kanban and material kanban arrive at the kanban post, the shear operation starts, and press operations follow.

159

Exhibit 11.11. Example of Signal and Material Kanban

Example of Material Kanban

Exhibit 11.12. Combined Use of Signal and Material Kanban

Note: Since shearing takes very little time, material kanban is used to get raw
material and store it next to the shear (①). Only when signal kanban
for the corresponding part arrives at the kanban post (②), is this raw
material processed.

With this arrangement, we can avoid starting the shear process earlier than necessary.

Move cards are used for delivery of parts in such areas as assembly lines, where delivery should be made just in time for assembly.

While the fabrication line may move one part through different processes, the assembly line typically withdraws parts from multiple locations for different processes. Therefore, move cards are used for this purpose (Exhibit 11.13).

Exhibit 11.13. Types of Information on a Move Kanban Card

(Example of Move Kanban)

Process (From)	Storage Location	C-2-3		Process (To)
Factory A	Part No.	17634-22631-12		Factory B
	Name of Part	Piston Ring		
Shipping Post No.	Container Type	S10	No. Issued	Receiving Post No.
Press 107	Container Capacity	200	3/5	Assembly 18

Example:
Red = Assembly Line
Blue = Paint
Black = Moulding
Orange = Press

(orange) (red)

Note: By designating colors for different lines, the handling of Kanban will be easier with fewer materials.

In Exhibit 11.14, examples of kanban and material routes are shown. As parts are consumed at the assembly line (1), move cards will be returned to the upstream process X (2). At the parts storage area of process (B), the move card will be exchanged for a production card and parts will be delivered to the assembly parts storage area A (3).

Exhibit 11.14. Use of Move Cards at Assembly Line Linked with Single-Card System in Fabrication Processes

Use of single card system for fabrication processes

Use of move card for parts supply to assembly line

Note: —— Material flow
----→ Kanban route

161

As the parts are delivered from parts storage area B, a production card will initiate production at process X (4) and finished parts will be stored at storage area B. In this fashion, the chain of events will follow the direction of the arrows in the exhibit.

Another point to be aware of is that the fabrication areas of Exhibit 11.14 depict a *single-card system*. At processes Y and Z, a production card serves the purpose of a move card as well (i.e., between parts storage areas D and C and between F and E) instead of adding move cards between those storage areas.

This arrangement makes sense when material moves through consecutive processes and there is little confusion about where the next process is. As a matter of fact, if processes X, Y, and Z are sequential and can be viewed as one process, one production card may serve the purpose. This type of kanban is often called tunnel kanban.

In-plant kanban are move cards used within a company. Supplier kanban are move cards used between manufacturers and suppliers. This is simply an extension of in-plant kanban to suppliers.

Number of Kanban and Improvement Opportunities

As mentioned before, the kanban system functions as a means to control production as well as to improve factory operations. Since kanban is merely a tool, the number of kanban cannot be determined by fixed formulas. The point is that kanban should help to expose problems in factory operations. In order to do this, the number of kanban cards should be reduced as much as possible so that inventory levels are reduced and problems exposed for improvement.

If we have a line with stable processes, for example, we should start to remove one kanban card at a time from the system. Since each card represents a predetermined quantity of a certain part in a container, we can reduce the level of work-in-process inventory of the part by reducing the number of cards. As long as we do not experience line stops due to parts shortages, the number of kanban cards can be reduced gradually until we hit a problem.

When a problem has been exposed, we should determine its source by asking "why" several times. Problems may be associated with machine maintenance, defects, container size, and the leveled/mixed production schedule. After a particular problem has been resolved and the line is stabilized again, we should eliminate another

kanban card for further improvement. This process is depicted in Exhibit 11.15.

Exhibit 11.15. Using Kanban for Continuous Improvement

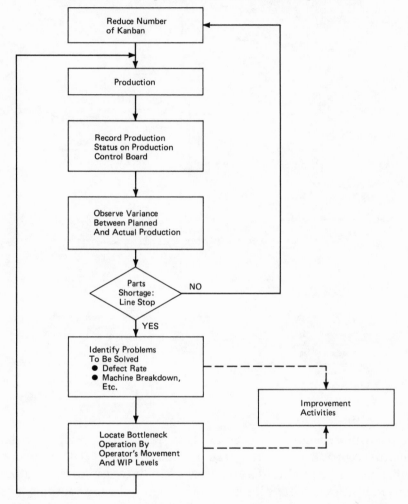

Examples

Supplier kanban. Material and kanban flows for a Japanese automobile manufacturer and one of its suppliers are described in Exhibit 11.16. Because of the many parts delivered to produce a variety of cars, a computer is used to determine the number of kanban required to obtain the necessary parts from suppliers. The appropriate

Exhibit 11.16. Flow of Material and Kanban Between Manufacturer and Supplier

Note:
→ Material and Kanban Flow
⇒ Material Flow
→ Kanban Flow
- - -→ Information Flow

* Monthly Production Plan:
Leveled/mixed production is
practiced on a monthly basis.
Accordingly, a leveled daily
production volume by product
types during the month (called
monthly production level) is
communicated to suppliers
for their planning purposes.

number will depend on the capability of the supplier, degree of leveled/mixed production, safety factors, and the like.* The number of kanban should be reduced as delivery cycles increase, or as lead time for preparation is reduced. On the other hand, the number may need to be increased if the leveled/mixed schedule is not maintained or the traffic situation is not predictable.

Exhibit 11.17 shows the kanban dispatch room of a Japanese automobile factory. In this factory, there are more than 10,000 sup-

*For a detailed calculation of number of kanban, please refer, for example, to Y. Monden, *Toyota Production System* (Institute of Industrial Engineers, Atlanta, 1983), Appendix 1.

Exhibit 11.17. Thousands of Supplier Kanban Cards waiting to Be Dispatched in a Japanese Automobile Factory

plier kanban cards circulated, corresponding to 97 percent of all items purchased outside. Because of the volume, an automated sorting machine is used to dispatch kanban cards to suppliers. The amount of the line-side stock in this assembly plant is about three hours.

Kanban squares. A Silicon Valley computer and electronics instrument manufacturer had spent more than three years of effort developing just-in-time when I visited their plants. In addition to their efforts to streamline the material flow, they emphasized the need for visual control and employee participation by implementing the kanban concept in a system they call "kanban squares."

The kanban square functions the same way as a kanban card, except that it does not use cards. A kanban square is an area designated to store in-process inventories. When there is predetermined amount of in-process inventory on the square, the operator in the upstream process will stop production; production restarts when the square is empty and continues until the square is full.

Exhibit 11.18. Use of Square Area as Kanban

The kanban square concept is also used in preparing printed circuit boards for large computers. As shown in Exhibit 11.19, racks are used as kanban. An operator in the upstream process fills each empty spot, and stops production when all of the racks are filled.

Exhibit 11.19. Use of Racks as Kanban in a Silicon Valley Company

Use of kanban in a tire plant. At a tire plant in Canada, the introduction of kanban has helped in reducing the work-in-process inventory level from twelve days to four days over a two-year period. In the same time period, the cost of quality, which is comprised of cost of scrap, rework, inspection, etc., went down from more than 11 percent to less than 6 percent of total sales.

Exhibit 11.20. History of Work-in-Process Inventory Level After Introduction of Kanban

At the bead manufacturing operation which produces the tire components, for example, the introduction of kanban has reduced the inventory level by 80 percent in four months.

We should remember, however, that kanban was not the single reason for these achievements. Involvement of people, workplace organization, setup time reduction, and statistical process control also contributed.

Use of kanban in a telecommunication equipment manufacturer. At a telecommunication equipment manufacturer on the West Coast, the introduction of kanban helped reduce the work-in-process inventory level from ten weeks to one week in a three-month period. As the inventory level dropped and linkages between operations

Exhibit 11.21. History of Work-in-Process Inventory Level and First Pass Rate After Introduction to Kanban

Work-in-Process Inventory

First-Pass Rate

Note: First-pass rate: percentage of good products completed without any rework.

tightened, more active communication took place among operators. As a result, the quality level went up significantly.

One of the major benefits of kanban is its user-friendliness. Operators are enthusiastic about kanban because of its simplicity and because they can control the schedule and feel a sense of ownership of production activities.

PRODUCTION CONTROL SYSTEM

A number of miscellaneous production control techniques can be used together with kanban. While monthly production levels and daily production plans may be developed with the leveled/mixed production concept, such tools as cycle tables, the reserved seat system, finished goods inventory status boards, kanban sequence tables, labels, the golf ball system, and the broadcast system are also used to fine tune the system (see Exhibit 11.22).

Whether or not production characteristics differ from automo-

Exhibit 11.22. Production Plan and Control System

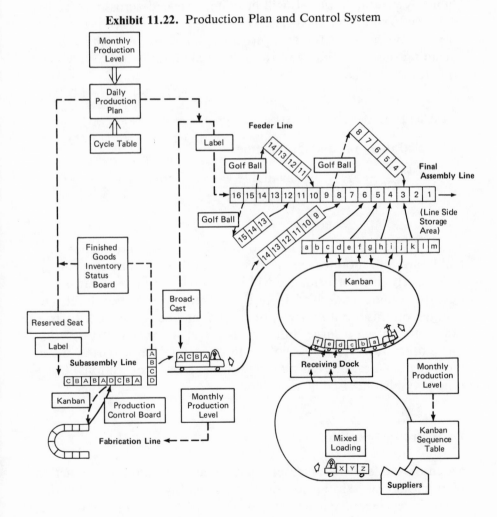

bile manufacturers or whether material requirements planning (MRP) is used for production control purposes, these techniques will help develop just-in-time production.

In the section below, we will examine in detail how these techniques are applied in a Japanese plant.

Monthly Production Level

If leveled/mixed production is practiced on a monthly basis, a leveled daily production volume by product type during the month (monthly production level) will be communicated across the factory and even to suppliers' factories. This information will serve as a guide to plan the capacity for each process. Standard work procedures, including the cycle time and the setup schedules, will be developed to enforce the plan.

Exhibit 11.23 Definition of Leveled Daily Production Volume and Cycle Time

$$\text{Leveled daily production volume} = \frac{\text{monthly production level}}{\text{working days}}$$

$$\text{Cycle time} = \frac{\text{available working hours/day}}{\text{leveled daily production volume}}$$

While kanban may be used to link processes, a production control board will monitor the production level of the line every hour. This hourly line performance will be compared to the planned production volume as derived from the monthly production level. Depending on this monthly level, operators may be reassigned. In Toyota's case, often a large number of operators are moved to other lines, other factories, or involved in quality circle activities, maintenance activities, or even training for quick setup operations. Overtime may also be used as a cushion.

Daily Production Plan

Based on the leveled/mixed production concept, a daily production plan should be developed for final assembly. For example, if a monthly leveled/mixed schedule is developed for four products, A,

B, C, and D, with production volumes of 4000, 3000, 2000, and 1000 units respectively, the production sequence may be developed as A-B-C-A-B-A-C-B-A-D, as indicated in Exhibit 11.24.

Exhibit 11.24. Development of Production Sequence

Product Type	Monthly Production Volume (units/mo.)	Daily Production Volume (units/day)	Cycle Time* (min/unit)	
A	4,000	200	2.5*	*500 min./shift are
B	3,000	150	3.3	assumed here
C	2,000	100	5.0	
D	1,000	50	10.0	
TOTAL	10,000	500	1.0*	

Product Type	Time (min.)										
	0	1	2	3	4	5	6	7	8	9	10
A			o			o		o			o
B				o			o				o
C						o					o
D											o

Production Sequence: A - B - C - A - B - A - C - B - A - D

In principle, kanban will pull materials from the rest of the plant to final assembly. Certain techniques which enforce leveled/mixed production help to execute kanban. The *cycle table* and *reserved seat/unreserved seat* concepts are examples of such techniques.

Cycle Table/Reserved Seat System

A leveled/mixed production schedule will prescribe a predetermined product mix for certain time periods. While kanban may link the processes and the production mix may be the same over time across the factory, the schedule may be disturbed as the distance from the final assembly line increases.

In order to reduce the chance of drifting away from leveled/mixed production at points further from the final assembly line, a cycle table may be developed to monitor and correct the shift from leveled/mixed production.

For example, if we know that the product mix is A = 40 percent, B = 30 percent, C = 20 percent, and D = 10 percent, a cycle table may be developed as A-B-A-C-B-A-C-B-A-D where ease of operation is also considered such that the time-consuming processes are

combined with less time-consuming processes—for example, C and D are separated since they are the most time-consuming items in this case.

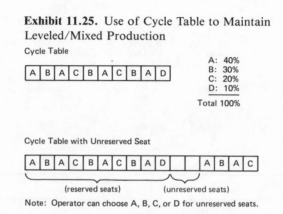

Exhibit 11.25. Use of Cycle Table to Maintain Leveled/Mixed Production

The kanban cards may be returned to the upstream process in a different sequence, such as B-A-A-C-C-D-A-B-B-A, or all at once. If we produce goods as the cards return, the original intent of leveled/mixed production schedule may not be realized since A, B, and C now may have a production lot of two or more rather than one. But if we use the cycle table as a base, such situations may be avoided.

As kanban cards return, they will be compared to the cycle table and if the cards match the sequence of the cycle table, work will be conducted according to that sequence. If a card for one item has not returned yet, we will skip that process and go to the next item on the cycle table. This preserves a sense of order similar to people with tickets who are looking for their reserved seats on a train or airplane. Because the sequence of returned kanban cards may not match the sequence of the cycle table, we provide one or two "unreserved seats" so that some flexibility can be maintained.

When one cycle has been completed, we will start again from the beginning. This means that when production volume increases, the turnaround time of the cycle table will be shortened. Also, if we find certain kanban cards accumulating or missing for production, we will know that the system needs adjustment such as a change in the product mix or lost kanban cards.

An example of the reserved/unreserved seating arrangement is shown in Exhibit 11.26.

In a painting or plating shop where hangers are used, the cycle table may be replaced by designating hangers according to a specific

Exhibit 11.26. Hanger Conveyors Used as Cycle Table

Note: Operator can choose A, B, C, or D for unreserved seats.

work sequence. Although many shops still do large batch production, the benefit of leveled/mixed production with a reserved/unreserved seating arrangement is worth investigating.

Finished Goods Inventory Status Board

In order to reflect actual sales, the status of finished goods inventory may be monitored and fed back to the production schedule. In some cases, the introduction of kanban between the finished goods inventory warehouse and the assembly line may be feasible. Generally speaking, however, such a practice is not advisable since it does not take the leveled/mixed production concept into consideration.

If we recall the analogy of kanban to a supermarket, this situation is similar to a customer buying a large amount of goods in a sporadic fashion. Our discussion on leveled/mixed scheduling emphasized smoothing the production schedule to protect the production efficiency from market fluctuations as much as reasonably possible. With leveled/mixed production, the final assembly line can consume parts in a steady fashion, helping the upstream process operations while quickly meeting fluctuating customer demands.

This same argument is applicable to some upstream processes, as the discussion of cycle tables and reserved/unreserved seating indicated. A *finished goods inventory status board* may also provide a way to handle the situation so that the principle of leveled/mixed production will not be violated.

In a subassembly line, manufacturing key components such as engines or transmissions for automobiles, finished goods are typically stored on conveyors by type before transfer to the final assembly line where the daily production plan is executed. Limit switches may be installed on conveyors to monitor the level of finished goods inventory by type. This information can then be displayed by product type on the finished goods inventory status board (see Exhibit 11.27).

Exhibit 11.27. Communicating Production Activity with Finished Goods Inventory Status Board

Product Type	Inventory Level 2 hr	4 hr	6 hr	8 hr	
36 GC					
36 GC1					
41 BC					
42 BC1					
45 AG	red	orange	yellow	green	blue

Note: A light will be lit corresponding to the level of inventory.

This information, along with the daily production plan, will contribute to a better production sequence.

Kanban Sequence Table

When large numbers of kanban cards are returned at once, as in the case of distant suppliers where the turnaround time is long, we need to develop ways to prioritize the work sequence. If these returned cards are not handled efficiently, several problems can arise.

For example, if certain items are produced in a consecutive sequence in large batches, there may be a parts shortage for those parts with low priority since there may be less chance of finishing all items on the kanban before the next shipping. In order to meet the shipping schedule, more inventory may be produced or unnecessary capacity may be needed. Also, if the work sequence is not carefully planned, the work content of different items may not be well combined to develop a balanced workload across the factory, resulting in line stoppages or unnecessary waiting time. Needless to say, the upstream processes may have similar problems.

To remedy this, a kanban sequence table may be used.

In Exhibit 11.28, returned kanban cards are sorted by product type and hung on the hooks from the left on the board. The board has three colors, green, yellow, and red, each indicating successive degrees of urgency. Since red is most urgent, production will be initiated by picking up the card from the far right of the board in the red color zone. A kanban sequence table used in a Canadian company is shown in Exhibit 11.29.

Exhibit 11.28. Use of a Kanban Sequence Table to Prioritize Work

Note: Green: not urgent
Yellow: less urgent
Red: urgent

Exhibit 11.29. A Kanban Sequence Table in a Canadian Company

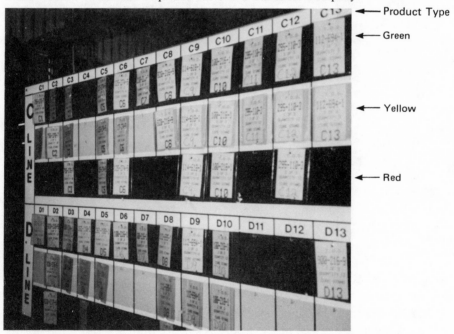

This board allows operators to judge the sequence of work. If we use actual lead time instead of color coding, the need for overtime can be estimated, and the potential of parts shortages will become quickly evident. While we have assumed the use of kanban cards here, the same concept may be applied using an electronic linkage between processes.

Labeling

In assembly operations with mixed/leveled production, various products may use different combinations of parts. In order to reduce confusion, labels are often used. An example of a label used in a Japanese automotive plant is shown in Exhibit 11.30, where each letter, number, or code corresponds to certain parts. The computer-generated label is attached to each workpiece, making it easy to distinguish parts even for newcomers (Exhibit 11.31).

Exhibit 11.30. Example of Label

The Golf Ball System

In the Exhibit 11.22 on production plan and control system, there are sixteen processes in the main assembly line and three feeder lines are linked to the main line with real golf balls. The golf balls are used to give operators the necessary production information at the right moment. When all operations in the feeder lines are completed, a component is ready to be assembled on time.

For example, when there are three processes 15, 14, and 13 in the feeder line and parts are assembled at process 12, it is sufficient

Exhibit 11.31. How Labels Are Used in an Automobile Assembly Line

to dispatch production information from process 15 of the main line to process 15 of the feeder line (see Exhibit 11.22). This is done with color-coded golf balls (see Exhibit 11.32) corresponding to different part numbers transmitted to the head of process 15 in the feeder line.

Obviously, we can do away with the golf balls and instead use electronic signals. For example, labels may be read by a bar-code

Exhibit 11.32. Use of Golf Ball System to Send Production Information

Note: Operator in the main line selects the golf ball as the label indicates. The operator in the feeder line then conducts operation as indicated by the golf ball. (Also see Exhibit 11.22)

reader and the corresponding operation may be indicated by a light panel with identifying symbols.

The Broadcast System

Similar to the golf ball system, the *broadcast system* is frequently used in the automobile industry. Information about the assembly sequence of vehicles is dispatched electronically and printed out at subassembly lines where transmissions, engines, and seats, are produced so that the same sequence of components will be transferred and arrive at the final assembly line in time.

This system is especially beneficial when there is a wide variety of products. For example, if more than seventy different kinds of transmissions or forty kinds of engines are assembled at the final assembly line, the line side storage requirement and inventory level will be too big to handle with kanban. By applying a broadcast system instead, the space and inventory levels will be significantly reduced and material handling improved.

The disadvantage of a broadcast system is that occasionally a sequence must be changed. For example, a single defect or delay of production information may confuse the whole system. For this reason, it is recommended that commonly used components be assembled in the upstream process and separate optional components be assembled in the downstream process where appropriate. With this change, the potential confusion caused by a broadcast system may be reduced.

SUMMARY

Tools such as kanban, cycle tables, kanban sequence tables, labels, golf balls, and broadcast system, can serve to link previously disjointed operations. They also help to eliminate overproduction. Goods are produced (and transferred) at the required time and in the required amount.

These tools may significantly improve operational efficiency for numerous manufacturing operations. It should be noted, however, that there should not be a limit to improving these tools themselves. For example, one of the benefits of kanban is that goods can carry with them the necessary operational information. In spite of this

benefit, however, the use of electronic communication may provide new methods to better serve the purpose.

Just as reducing the number of kanban cards will help us think of ways to generate improvement ideas, we should not be satisfied with the tools currently available. With a challenging spirit and creative thinking, we can improve these tools as well.

Chapter 12

Redefining the Roles of Conveyors and Transportation

In the previous chapter, we discussed various techniques to tie different activities together so that waste can be eliminated. While kanban, broadcast system, and other techniques will help significantly in doing this, we often overlook the importance of physical arrangements that support and complement these techniques. For example, we may view the roles of conveyors or trucks as merely those of transferring materials from one place to the next. Furthermore, we may think that once such systems are installed, nothing can be changed. This is especially true for most transportation systems since they usually require coordinating different functions in order to make any changes. However, as we have learned earlier, *simplify, combine,* and *eliminate* are three basic steps toward improvement. Now we will apply those ideas for the better use of conveyors as well as other transportation mechanisms.

CONVEYORS

From the days of Henry Ford, the conveyor has been considered a convenient vehicle to transfer materials and to help make the production process efficient. But unless conveyors are used carefully,

180

they can become a source of much waste. For example, we have seen much time wasted by operators picking and placing parts when using the conveyor. We have also seen lots of materials stored on conveyors. Furthermore, conveyors can be a source of waste by requiring more space and operators' time for walking and by making coordination between processes more difficult.

Generally speaking, there are two different types of conveyors. One is a stationary type with no power source to move materials on the conveyor. The other kind has a power source, for example, a motor that moves the workpieces on it at a certain speed. We will examine the application of each of these types of conveyors below.

Stationary Conveyors

This type of conveyor is often misused in storing parts and creating unnecessary problems. The following examples of its application will show us how the conveyor is often misused in factories.

Numerous examples of this type of application are found in various factories. Exhibit 12.1 shows four operators at machines A, B, C, and D, respectively. On the conveyor, parts are stacked on containers.

Exhibit 12.1. Common Misapplication of Stationary Conveyors for Machining Line

This layout, however, is preferable to one in which the four machines are placed in different locations, requiring long transportation distances that make it difficult to coordinate activities (see Exhibit 12.2). Such an arrangement may result in much more inventory

Exhibit 12.2. Inefficient Machine Layout

stacked on the floor, more transportation waste, and wasted motion in picking and placing parts.

Exhibit 12.1 is therefore considered an improvement over Exhibit 12.2. But we should always remind ourselves that there is no end to our improvement activities. As we saw in chapter 6 (pages 69–89), if we look closely at this arrangement, we may find such waste as the following:

1. Operators are spending a large portion of their time pushing and pulling the parts containers on the conveyor, picking and placing parts, and walking between the conveyor and the machines.
2. The conveyor's layout often makes it difficult to coordinate different kinds of work. Therefore, operators may be idle while they watch a machine finish processing.
3. Since large amounts of inventory tend to accumulate between processes, the operators are shielded from each other. As a result, when one operator finds defects from the previous operation, many parts will have to be reworked or scrapped.
4. The inventory accumulation hinders communication among operators. Each operator works at his own pace, making it difficult to tell who is the busiest or where the bottlenecks are in the line.

To eliminate as much of this waste as possible, we may be able to install a U-shaped line such as that shown in Exhibit 12.3.

Exhibit 12.3. Rearrangement to U-Shaped Layout After Improvement

(Note: As discussed before, if operator cannot be separated from the machine operation, think of a way to solve it by incorporating jidoka ideas.)

The idea is to achieve one-piece flow production. In this case, two operators follow each other, each operating four machines. The inventory in the process has now been reduced significantly to one piece per machine. The conveyor has been disposed of altogether and the production lead time and quality level have improved significantly.

Exhibit 12.4. Use of Stationary Conveyor for Assembly Line

Many assembly lines have an arrangement similar to the machining line described in Exhibit 12.1, where each operation is separated from the other operations. The waste of pick and place motion is substantial in this arrangement as well. The difference in each operator's skill or the differences in work content of each operation will create an unsteady flow of materials resulting in an accumulation of inventory on the conveyor.

One remedial approach is to limit the in-process inventory between operations, for example, to a maximum of two. With this method, we can identify problem areas by observing the inventory level on the conveyor and exposing excessive operator waiting time. Exposing a problem is the first major step in solving it. A more powerful approach is, of course, one piece-flow production. By simplifying the operation, and having operators stand rather than sit, we

generally find a vast improvement. Another option may be to use motor-driven conveyors, especially when the material to work on is heavy or bulky.

Motor-Driven Conveyors

The major features of motor-driven conveyors are as follows:

1. The speed of the conveyor can be used to provide a rhythm for operators in their work. In order to do this, however, workpieces should be placed at equal intervals.
2. A conveyor that can move at variable speeds will provide a capability to adjust the speed and manning requirements according to demand changes.
3. This type of conveyor makes it possible to transfer and work on parts at the same time. Wherever possible, conveyors should not be used solely for transportation.

In order to use conveyors in a just-in-time fashion, a few conditions must be met.

1. Transfer only the amount of materials required by the next process.
2. Transfer materials at predetermined intervals. (This concept is tied to the notion of cycle time control as discussed in Chapter 9.)
3. If problems arise, the conveyor should be able to be stopped quickly.

The following examples will explain these points in more detail.

In Exhibit 12.5, workpieces are moved at a steady speed. The intervals between workpieces are kept the same as shown by the dotted lines. Each interval corresponds to the cycle time.

Besides the conveyor, there are line stop marks that indicate where the conveyor stops when there is a delay of work by any operator in the line. Electric interlocks are set so that the conveyor will stop at the points where pitch marks and line stop marks meet.

In this example, when operator A or H has no work, subsequent operations cannot be conducted. Therefore, the conveyor should stop. We call this a "no work" situation.

On the other hand, when operator G or N has completed his

Exhibit 12.5. Use of Motor-Driven Conveyor for Assembly Line

*Line Stop Mark: When conveyor stops, it should stop where the pitch mark and line stop mark meet so that the impact to operators is minimal.

work but the workpiece is not carried away to the next process, inventory will accumulate and confusion will result. Therefore, the conveyor should stop in this case, too. We call this a "full work" situation.

Furthermore, when there are work delays at any operation caused by lack of parts, defective parts, or operational difficulty, the line should be stopped at certain designated points where the operators' work is least affected—that is, the line stop mark should correspond to the end of the work cycle. (See Chapter 7 for a discussion of the line stop concept.) The sequence of line stopping and its relationship to the display on an andon panel are as follows.

1. The operator will push a stop button if quality problems or lack of parts lead to a delay in work.
2. A yellow andon light will be turned on to signal a supervisor. The conveyor, however, will not stop suddenly but continue to move at its normal rate.
3. A supervisor will arrive for assistance. If the problem is resolved in time with the supervisor's help, the stop button switch will be reset by the supervisor and the conveyor will keep moving.
4. If the problem cannot be resolved, however, the conveyor will be stopped at a designated point and a red andon light will be turned on.

Note: In emergency situations, however, the line can be stopped immediately.

One of the biggest benefits of this line stop procedure is that problems on the line are exposed, catching the supervisors' attention and initiating problem-solving activities.

An equally important feature is the development of teamwork between operators and supervisors. When operators and supervisors work together to achieve the same goal for the organization, a favorable environment for continuous improvement tends to be created.

The next example describes the case where workpieces are moved by conveyor in a stop-and-go fashion.

In Exhibit 12.6, the operator presses a switch when the work is completed. This releases a stopper and allows the workpiece to move to the next station by roller-flight conveyor. Some might think it necessary to conduct the operation with the workpiece held still. However, this arrangement proves troublesome in the long run because of difficulties in exposing problems and identifying areas for improvement. These difficulties stem from a lack of cycle time concept. As mentioned before, without the use of cycle time as a standard, it is difficult to make improvements.

Exhibit 12.6. Use of Roller-Flight Conveyor for Assembly Line

There are, however, several ways to solve this problem. For example, we can:

- determine the maximum practical inventory level between processes, and set an interlock to prevent excessive buildup
- provide an interlock tied to all operators' push buttons as well as to a timer that monitors cycle time so that all workpieces will be released when all of these conditions are met
- use an andon light and/or buzzer to indicate the elapsed time for each operation

An even better method may be to conduct the operation without the use of a stopper. If operators are properly trained, and tools,

product design, and work procedures are improved, use of a constant speed conveyor generally produces better results in the long run because of the ease in identifying problems with the cycle time control concept.

TRANSPORTATION

The transportation of materials for production must be considered in conjunction with the production process. Whether transportation takes place within the plant or between manufacturers and suppliers, we often find disorder and waste created because of inappropriate attention to transportation activities. Even though timing, volume, and distance of transportation may vary in each setting, transportation simply ties together processes from raw material to fabrication, or final assembly to shipping at the rate required by the market.

We discussed this idea earlier in regard to use of a U-shaped line with cycle time control to keep the production flow steady. This is also the same idea we examined regarding the use of a conveyor to develop the constant flow of workpieces.

If we can tie all production operations with an "invisible conveyor", producing one piece at a time, and transporting one piece at a time as required by the next process, we would have the ideal production system. If we view inventory as waste, then transportation may be viewed as a way to accumulate inventory on the move—which is, of course, undesirable.

In Exhibit 12.7, transportation is simulated by valves connecting separate pools of inventory in manufacturing processes. If pressure builds up for too long before the valve is opened, the discharge of

Exhibit 12.7. Transportation Functions as a Valve in a Water System

Note:
Transportation can be considered similar to a valve. If not controlled well, it creates intermittent glut of material flow.

inventory is similar to a discharge of water from a dam in the spring season.

Transferring materials in large batch sizes creates a glut of material flow in a disorderly fashion. The question for us is: "How can we come close to developing a piece-by-piece transportation flow without incurring excessive transportation costs?" We will try to answer this question below.

In-Plant Transportation

If we develop a production line as the material flows, it is possible to develop one-piece flow production. In such an arrangement, when one process stops, the whole line stops. As a result, we can identify problems and focus our activities on problem solving and improving production processes. If the processes are far apart, the physical distance often makes it difficult to link them with an appropriate level of communication.

Even in such a case, however, we should seek to have transportation play the role of the conveyor. The goal of transportation is, again, to transfer the required materials at the required time in the required quantity. This can be accomplished if the following conditions are met:

- Frequent delivery
- Frequent feedback of information from the next process concerning quality problem, and priority of work
- No storage in between the processes
- Mixed loading of required materials as appropriate
- Efforts to reduce transportation costs

In order to meet these conditions, a few points need to be addressed further:

1. Transportation is based on the requirement of the next process. If the next process is not ready to receive material(s), there should be no transportation.
2. To reflect this, the transportation function should be under the control of the next process.
3. The amount of materials transported should also be determined by the amount required in the same time period by the next process. If this is not practiced, leveled production cannot be maintained throughout the plant.

4. In order to keep the transportation batch size as small as possible, and the transportation low in cost, mixed loading may be practiced. To reduce waste associated with double handling, etc., a one-touch or easy handling method such as the method shown in Exhibit 12.8 may be developed.

Exhibit 12.8. Mixed Loading and One-Touch Handling Methods

Plant-to-Plant Transportation

When materials are transferred by truck over long distances, such as between a supplier's plant and the manufacturer's plant, certain additional considerations are usually required.

In this case, we tend to think it is more efficient to use a large truck to transfer one kind of product between the two locations. This may be true if we consider only the transportation function. But the role of transportation is to help production activities with the minimum amount of inventory, tying two plants with an "invisible conveyor system." Materials transfer should be synchronized with other production activities. To achieve this, multiplant transportation with mixed loading is often recommended. Exhibit 12.9 shows the benefits of mixed loading/multiplant transportation as compared to a single plant-to-plant transportation pattern. It is obvious here that the mixed loading pattern has several benefits over the conventional method:

- Because of frequent deliveries, inventory levels in the manufacturer's and supplier's plants can be kept low.
- This helps reduce the size of the inventory storage area and the number of pallets.
- When defects are found, immediate action can be taken to minimize the damage.
- Since information from the next process can be fed back more frequently, the upstream process is less likely to produce the wrong or unnecessary products.

Exhibit 12.9. Benefits of Mixed Loading/Multiplant Transportation

- Even if there is a delay in the upstream process, it may be possible to wait for the next truck rather than dispatching another truck.

When two plants are far away from each other, a warehouse may be established in between. Since there are several problems associated with this approach (such as double or triple handling of materials, necessary space, inventory and parts obsolescence), direct transportation between plants should be utilized as much as possible. Some of the benefits of direct transportation are:

- Elimination of the warehouse, unnecessary inventory, and material handling.
- Frequent and early feedback of information from the next process (i.e., low information inventory).
- Reduced risk of defective products because feedback is prompt.

Receiving Incoming Materials

When frequent deliveries are received from suppliers, some trucks may deliver directly to the point of use in the plant; others may deliver to receiving docks. Delivery to the point of use is ideal in eliminating unnecessary double handling. In Exhibit 12.10, automobile seats are carried by truck to the point of use in an assembly line in Japan. With the use of a gravity conveyor, the time to unload thirty sets of seats is only a few minutes. Delivery is made every 30 minutes from the nearby supplier.

Exhibit 12.10. Delivery of Materials Directly to the Line

Deliveries can also be made to receiving docks where a number of trucks can be unloaded at short time intervals. Especially when frequent deliveries are desired in line with the just-in-time philosophy, we need to find the most efficient way to schedule deliveries and simplify receiving activities.

The major factor in an efficient receiving operation is the leveled schedule. In Exhibit 12.11, receiving activity is not leveled. Therefore, even though production at the next process is leveled, we can assume that unnecessary inventory is accumulated somewhere in the production processes.

Unleveled receiving operations also require additional people at peak delivery periods, as well as additional storage space, pallets,

Exhibit 12.11. Unleveled Loads Lead to Inefficient Receiving Operations

forklifts, and waiting time for truck drivers. A typical approach in developing a leveled schedule is first to set up delivery periods for trucks coming from far away and then schedule the trucks coming from nearby. This may be controlled by a receiving control board (as opposed to a production control board) as shown in Exhibit 12.12.

Exhibit 12.12. Receiving Control Board

Time	Name of Co.			Comment
8:00 - 9:00	A	B	E —(Green)	
9:00 - 10:00	A	C	F	F had flat tire (delay of 20 min)
10:00 - 11:00	A	B	G — (White)	
11:00 - 12:00	A	D	H	

Note: As the delivery is made, the card corresponding to the company will be turned over so that visual control is easy (white: not arrived; green: arrived).

Note that a prescheduled trucking plan will result in underutilizing truck capacity. That is, when the next processes have line stops, the quantities to be transferred will be reduced. Therefore, constant-volume/variable-time transportation as practiced in-plant and variable-volume/constant-time transportation as practiced plant-to-plant should be examined carefully, considering the distance of transportation and other factors.

Lastly, in order to conduct receiving operations quickly and effectively, workplace organization of the receiving dock becomes important. For example, color coding and numbering for different locations may be a first step for improvement.

Example: Reduction of Transportation Cost

In a trucking operation between the plants of a Japanese automobile manufacturer, truck drivers were often idle for long periods during loading and unloading. By adding two additional trucks to one trucking loop system, this company has saved more than $100,000 annually. (There are tens of similar systems functioning in this company.)

At the manufacturer and at supplier B in Exhibit 12.13, trucks are waiting ready to go for the next driver. When the drivers of trucks 2 and 5 arrive at those locations, they will leave their trucks and move to trucks 3 and 6. Trucks 2 and 5 will then be unloaded and loaded again so that they are ready for the next drivers, and so on.

Exhibit 12.13. Drivers' Time is Better Utilized by Adding More Trucks

While the utilization of trucks declines under the new system—compared to the traditional one-driver/one-truck relationship—the driver's time is better utilized by reducing waiting time. As a result, this approach is typically much more economical in spite of the expense in purchasing additional trucks.

It is worth noting that the total annual savings of millions of dollars results from increasing the productive use of the drivers' time alone, and does not reflect additional savings from reduced inventories and space requirements. (Recall that we discussed a similar

idea in Chapter 6: Multiple-process handling of machines in a U-shaped line often results in significant savings even though machine utilization rates may go down.)

The factories in this example are located within twenty miles of each other, and the interval between trucking deliveries is about half an hour. Thus transportation links factories closely together and helps to serve the production process as an invisible conveyor.

Exhibit 12.14 shows a truck with side-loading feature used in Japan. This type of truck provides easy handling of materials, making it easy to mix loads for multiple deliveries and/or multiple pick-ups, contributing to lower-cost transportation.

Exhibit 12.14. Side-Loading Truck Helps Provide Easy Access to Materials

SUMMARY

In this chapter, we discussed conveyors and transportation mechanisms and how they link production activities.

First, we addressed the inefficiencies often associated with the use of conveyors. Conveyors are frequently used as storage points for accumulating inventories. The pick and place activities associated with conveyors can waste operators' time, as can inefficient movement of materials. Much of the waste associated with conveyors can

be eliminated by rearranging layouts, or by making better use of the conveyors by, for example, introducing the line stop concept.

Second, in reviewing the role of transportation, we pointed out that people directly involved with transportation should not be optimizing their own operations without paying attention to the total production activities. Transportation should be viewed as an "invisible conveyor," promoting a smooth flow of material. To serve this purpose we should develop a policy of frequent transportation and leveled transportation scheduling at minimum cost.

Suppliers as Extended Factories

We have, thus far, focused on the improvement activities internal to a manufacturing organization. In order to increase a company's manufacturing competitiveness, however, supplier relationships need to be incorporated into the total picture. We have reviewed the importance of developing a smooth flow of material and information across the factory through such means as reducing setup time and instituting leveled/mixed production. We then examined the importance of tying things together rather than focusing on individual efforts. Similarly, a manufacturer's relationships with suppliers can improve the company's performance multifold by addressing the total manufacturing system rather than concentrating on the individual company's practices.

This is especially true when a company's competitors are not pursuing better supplier relationships. We should recognize that competition is not simply a matter of one company trying to dominate others in the industry. Rather, it is often a matter of one group of companies functioning as an integrated manufacturing system competing with another group of companies.

If one group does not work closely together, but its competitor's group is working together to maximize its power as a group, how can it succeed? If one group shares ideas for better working relationships in such fields as design, manufacturing, and logistics, and the other group does not, what will be the outcome?

NEW SUPPLIER RELATIONSHIPS

We have already discussed improvement activities in such areas as machines, layout, schedule, production control, and job rotation. The evaluation of suppliers should reflect on all the points discussed before. If we think of our manufacturing operation as an economic system, the evaluation process should not be limited to a single component of that system. Instead, manufacturers and suppliers should work together to develop an integrated manufacturing system by eliminating the wastes that are typically accumulated between these organizational boundaries.

Some important considerations are the following:

1. From the supplier's point of view, manufacturers are customers. Suppliers should guarantee *delivery, quality,* and *cost* to the manufacturers. They should work closely to understand and incorporate the manufacturer's requirements in their services.
2. In the delivery area, frequent, small lot, on-time deliveries should be targeted in order to make the manufacturer-supplier linkages tighter. To do this, application of a kanban system between manufacturer and supplier, mixed loading, and frequent deliveries of materials may be practiced.
3. In the quality area, the idea of "quality at the source" should be practiced as much as possible. Use of poka-yoke and statistical process control should be encouraged as these are practiced in the manufacturer's factory.
4. In the cost area, improvement activities similar to those in the manufacturer's factory should take place. Sharing ideas for cost improvements will help secure the companies' competitive position.

In the following part of this section, we will look into each of these areas in more detail.

Delivery

In the area of delivery, efforts should be devoted to developing a steady flow of materials from supplier to manufacturer. This idea is quite similar to developing "flow" within the factory as discussed earlier.

In the factory, rearranging machine layouts and installing small dedicated equipment can simplify and smooth the material flow. If we apply these concepts to the suppliers, at least two points become clear.

1. Having dedicated suppliers for production of certain parts is just like arranging machines for a dedicated material flow. It reduces confusion, increases operational linkages, and facilitates improvements.

Exhibit 13.1. Comparison of Multiple and Single-Source Supplier Arrangements

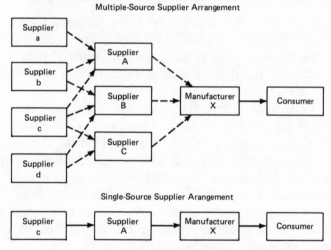

The most dependable, cooperative suppliers should be identified and a close working relationship should be developed functioning as an ''extended factory'' from the manufacturer's point of view. A large-scale supplier is not necessarily a dependable, cooperative supplier. Rather, large suppliers may have so many customers that one manufacturer's share of their business may be too small to influence their behavior or to persuade them to develop a mutually beneficial arrangement.

Just as a multipurpose super machine may not fit well into an efficient manufacturing system, a large multipurpose supplier may not be as appropriate as a production system dedicated to the manufacturer in the supplier's factory.

2. Having suppliers close to the manufacturer improves the relationship between the two.

Just as the physical arrangement of machines influences productivity, so do the quality and delivery from the supplier's location impact upon the manufacturer's performance. First of all, physical distance will influence the transportation batch size and the frequency of transportation. Even though there are ways to reduce the batch size and increase the frequency of transportation, such as by a mixed loading truck arrangement, closer suppliers will have advantages over more distant suppliers.

Exhibit 13.2. Mixed Loading and Rearranged Transportation Patterns

Needless to say, reduced storage areas, elimination of double and triple handling, frequent feedback of information, quick adjustments of abnormal conditions, and reduced inventories are some of the benefits of frequent small batch transportation from suppliers.

In addition to material transportation problems, distant suppliers may be at a disadvantage in communication because of the less frequent visits by their personnel. Especially in the early phase of developing a close supplier relationship, cross visitation may be most helpful in tying distant operations together. People from purchasing, production, quality assurance, and engineering need to participate in developing a reliable, cooperative, long-term working relationship.

Physical distance makes it more difficult to develop face-to-face contacts. Letters, reports, or phone conversations cannot provide the benefit of "visual control" which is only possible during actual visits to the plant.

Quality

The "quality at the source" concept should be practiced on the supplier's side as well as the manufacturer's side.

Exhibit 13.3. Stages of Progress Toward "Quality at the Source"

Stages of Progress	Manufacturer		Supplier		Additional Cost Passed to the Customer
	Production	Incoming Inspection	Outgoing Inspection	Production	
1	○	○			($)
2		○	○		
3		∘	○		
4		∘	○	∘	
5			∘	○	
6			Poka–Yoke/Process Control	○	

Note: Circles indicate the importance of quality check-points for the material produced by suppliers.

As indicated in Exhibit 13.3, the earlier the detection of problems, the lower the cost to the customer. There will be less rework, less scrap, less disruption to the schedule, and fewer resources wasted.

In principle, the approach to this is the same as that used in our own factory, except that the organizational barriers between manufacturers and suppliers are often hard to break, especially at the beginning.

As with other areas of improvement, if a company is not yet practicing supplier development, how can it compete effectively with those who have developed close relationships to improve quality together? For instance, consider Toyota, where the majority of parts delivered from suppliers are used without incoming inspection. If your company is doing 100 percent incoming inspection and your competitor has achieved non-incoming inspection for the majority of parts, such as Toyota did, what option does your company have?

Cost

When the number of suppliers is reduced, and an arm's length relationship turns into a closer, friendlier relationship, cost improvement activities can be practiced much more easily. With a shared understanding, both parties will develop an idea of codestiny through

helping each other, and practicing things which make the most sense for both of them.

As described before, transportation and delivery methods will be reconsidered, and quality assurance activities will be focused at the source. These activities will help to improve the cost position for both parties in competing with other companies in the business. Furthermore, there are many other approaches to help reduce product costs. These activities include the early involvement of suppliers in product development, cross visitation to share productivity improvement activities, and joint study teams to share improvement programs.

In the section below, we will see a few examples of these activities.

Examples

Suppliers' day. From a computer manufacturer in Silicon Valley to a motorcycle manufacturer on the East Coast, progressive companies are incorporating their suppliers' abilities into their manufacturing strategies. After realizing the importance of developing a strategic alliance with suppliers, these companies came up with ways to evaluate suppliers' capabilities for their new relationship with them. Hosting a suppliers' day is an effective way to kick off and to pursue this.

To begin suppliers' day, for example, the manufacturer's top management people might present their views on competition, market trends, and the need to develop closer relationships with suppliers in order to remain competitive.

Areas of potential improvement in quality, cost, and delivery of the supplier's product should be presented together with proposals for exploring these potential improvements. Some of the proposals might include a supplier evaluation program, study groups, education and training programs, exchange visits, early involvement of suppliers for product design, and perhaps a new trucking program. Another agenda for suppliers' day may be a visit to the manufacturer's plant so that visitors can observe improvement activities.

With this agenda, a manufacturer can convey its vision of the future where new relationships with suppliers are to evolve, rather than maintaining the traditional relationship through contracts and occasional phone calls.

Supplier evaluation program and selection of suppliers. As a step toward developing a closer relationship and forming a strategic alliance with key suppliers, a supplier evaluation program should be conducted.

In the long run, this will lead to a much smaller number of strategically important suppliers than is found in the conventional arrangement where price negotiation is a major factor in selecting suppliers. This may be viewed as a tradeoff between a short-term profit-taking orientation and a long-term involvement where the benefits may come from all aspects of the close relationship. From quality information to cooperative cost reduction activities, or from eliminating unnecessary paperwork to coordinating design activities, this new form of relationship requires trust and openness in pursuing the goal of coprosperity.

The Q1 award by Ford is an award given to suppliers under this certification program, the goal of which is to select fewer suppliers and to do business with them exclusively. General Motors has a similar program called Source Performance Education and Reporting (SPEAR).

One criterion for evaluating suppliers that should not be overlooked is the supplier's own management philosophy. Exhibit 13.4 summarizes several types of evaluation criteria. While there is no single approach, evaluating suppliers on each item and ranking suppliers on a point system are approaches often used in Japan. Obviously, this type of evaluation may be conducted at regular intervals.

Exhibit 13.4. Checklist for Supplier Evaluation (Example)

Policy	Sales volume
Management philosophy	Degree of mutual dependency
Education and training	Current position in quality, cost, and delivery
Managerial capability	Control systems for quality, cost, and delivery
Financial capability	Improvement activities
Equipment capability	Future plans
Technical capability	Level of commitment and understanding of our
Product development capa-	approaches
bility	Others
Quality assurance	
Employee/union relationship	
Location	

Other programs with suppliers. Manufacturers may send their quality assurance or engineering people to assist their suppliers; production control people from both companies may work together to streamline the production flow; improvement teams from various companies may visit a host plant to participate in a two-day improvement activity at the shop floor.

The point is, again, that suppliers should be thought of as "extended factories." Even though there may be physical boundaries between companies, we should first think about the economic needs of production.

SUMMARY

We have discussed the needs and approaches to develop a new cooperative relationship with suppliers where both manufacturer and suppliers can prosper. Instead of simply maintaining an arms-length, contractual relationship with suppliers, the manufacturer should think of the suppliers as an extension of the factory.

This notion becomes especially important when we see more business competition taking place in a fashion such that one group of companies is competing with another group of companies. If a supplier network is so weak for one group of companies that communication between manufacturer and suppliers is not well established, problems associated with quality, delivery, and cost will hurt not only the manufacturer but the suppliers as well.

The point is that we need to be able to see the broader picture of value-added chain of events, from acquisition of raw materials (natural resources in some cases) to distribution and use of product at the customer's end. Then, by looking for wastage points in this value-added chain and eliminating them through practicing the idea of "simplify, combine, and eliminate," we will find opportunities for improvement. Co-destiny, co-survival, and co-prosperity are simply a result of these efforts.

Chapter 14

Developing Co-Destiny with Employees

Whether or not the factory is unionized, the involvement of all employees and the development of shared goals among them are the keys to success. The more developed the people's skills, the stronger the company's capabilities. The more information is shared and the more workers are educated and/or trained, the less trouble there will be to develop common goals and make improvements for the organization.

In this chapter, we will discuss how to achieve the goals of the organization by developing co-destiny with employees.

JOB SECURITY

Job security is obviously a strong concern for employees. If an employee offered a labor-saving suggestion and a colleague was laid off because of it, how would he feel about it? There would be no trust for managers who take such actions.

Also, if employees' abilities are not utilized to the fullest extent, how can a company compete effectively with rival companies that encourage employee suggestions and involvement, and utilize people's resources effectively to gain more business? If everyone's cooperation is not obtained, does it make any sense to hire consultants or additional staff/support people to come up with ideas?

The point is that in all of the industries in which I have worked, there is no effective cost-benefit relationship that does not involve developing human resources. It makes more sense to develop and utilize the workers' ability to improve performance and maintain job security rather than to rely on extra staff, management, and consultants and risk alienating other workers. Most Japanese companies seem to have learned this simple yet important lesson years ago.

A Position for Everybody

Employees whose positions are eliminated as a result of improvement activities should be moved to where their skills are most suited, or they can be re-educated or trained to develop new skills. People with knowledge of machines may be positioned to work on machine improvement or in the machine selection process. Employees with skills in quality control may become trainers of statistical process control. Some people with production backgrounds may even visit customers as sales people to sell more products or assist engineers in developing new products.

We cannot simply assume that an individual's ability will not change over time. With appropriate opportunities to fulfill their potential through education, training, and other programs, people have unlimited potential. Often, however, these precious resources are not explored because of outdated systems, rigid structures, and insensitive management attitudes. As in the case of improved supplier relationships described in the previous chapter, people's skills can be significantly increased given the appropriate management attention. As the relationships with suppliers change toward a closer relationship rather than negotiation based on price, the position of the people *within* the firm needs to be redefined.

IMPROVEMENT THROUGH PEOPLE

I believe that everybody can contribute something to improve the quality of work. Nevertheless, in many companies the reward systems and structures do not seem to have addressed this point well. As a result, there is typically a lack of motivation or incentive for improvement.

I view the number of suggestions offered by employees as a good

measure of the direct link between improvement and motivation. Yet I have observed many cases where suggestion programs are dormant or inoperable as a result of a cumbersome and overly long evaluation process, or because employees feel they cannot trust their managers. If we compare these companies with companies like Toyota, whose employees generate millions of suggestions every year, with an adoption rate of over 90 percent, how can these companies compete?

If we subscribe to the idea that viability in business is tied to improvement and improvement is tied to employee motivation, we should reconsider the meaning of improvement to the people in the factory. Depending on the situation, "improvement" for these people may mean: (1) more business, (2) lay-offs, (3) early retirement, (4) hiring freeze, (5) reduction of temporary workers, (6) allocation of resources to new business development, (7) production of previously purchased parts in house, or some combination of these.

In the following examples, we will study how different companies are dealing with these difficult yet crucial issues.

Example

Omark Industries and Hewlett-Packard may be considered two of the advanced companies in the United States in terms of implementing just-in-time and total quality control concepts. Even though Omark and Hewlett-Packard are in different businesses, each of them has shown similar characteristics toward its employees.

While Omark has announced that the company will not lay off their people through improvement activities, Hewlett-Packard virtually guarantees no layoffs as its policy. One of Omark's general managers, for example, has diversified into new businesses to utilize his factory's increased capability resulting from JIT/TQC improvement activities.

Hewlett-Packard, on the other hand, implements across-the-board pay cuts when their business goes down. For example, they instituted a 10 percent pay cut during the computer and instrumentation industry slump in 1985. Hewlett-Packard management shares with its employees the notion that "we are all in the same boat."

These two companies are making headway in establishing co-destiny between company and the employees. In these companies, the boundary between the company and their employees seems to be

gradually fading away in the process of developing a new industrial democracy.

Example

A 1700-employee plant of a Big Three automobile manufacturer has been attempting to develop a close relationship with the union for the last several years. Initially, progress was slow. Many positive thinkers, however, kept working together to get the message across. For example, the plant manager started to pick up trash from the floor. Open communication was viewed as a key, and the dining room and parking areas were opened to all employees.

The hourly employees are called Quality Operators here. They work in teams of twelve to fifteen members. The Team Coordinators are the equivalent of line supervisors, and retain overall responsibility for quality, productivity, safety, training, and other aspects of the production process. Thus, the "autonomous" team concept was introduced in this organization.

A former Team Coordinator comments, "Who knows the job better than the man or woman who does it all day? Traditionally, the boss doesn't want to give up control, but here we know the hourly worker is closer to the situation. So we give him or her broader responsibility and ask them to use their own judgement in their work."

After the autonomous team concept was introduced, the number of union grievances declined from a hundred to one per month. Currently, employees contribute about 400 suggestions a month and the adoption rate is reasonably high. Jobs are rotated within the teams, with members deciding on how frequently these rotations occur.

In the production area, the previous forty-seven job classifications were reduced to one with a "pay-for-knowledge" system, where wages are determined more by the skills or knowledge of people rather than seniority. Training is considered an important activity tied to the pay-for-knowledge system. Close to $2 million is spent annually on the program.

The plant's personnel administrator comments, "It is amazing how people respond when given the opportunity. We in management have to realize that we have a vast, largely untapped resource in our work force. Properly stimulated, this resource will work wonders in contributing to quality and productivity."

Example

At a Canadian tire company of about 1500 employees, union contract negotiations focused recently on problems associated with middle management.

Operators believed that although supervisors and middle management people controlled almost everything about their daily work, they rarely really listened to the operators. In such an environment, trust between management and the operators had been difficult to develop. Even though top management had been advocating participative management, middle management resisted changing.

Throughout the contract negotiation and the informal discussions, the union's focal point was this issue. The crucial point seemed to be whether or not management would listen to the operators' opinions frequently and take actions promptly.

While there were no clear-cut resolutions to this situation, this factory is viewed as one of the best managed North American tire manufacturing facilities. Quality and productivity have improved through the introduction of statistical process control and just-in-time production techniques. The next step is to change the way middle management and the operators work together.

SUMMARY

Even though this is one of the shortest chapters in the book, its subject, together with topics in Chapters 15 and 16 on teamwork and people involvement, is of paramount importance for the future of many Western manufacturing industries. Even though the degree of criticalness may vary from industry to industry, or company to company, the common thread is a humanistic approach to management and the need to eliminate waste. In fact, I would add an eighth waste to the list of seven wastes developed at Toyota (Chapter 1): the waste of underutilized people's skills and capabilities.

With regard to the union situation specifically, job security and mobility of operators with multiple skills are the key to better relationships. Many Japanese companies have developed friendly relationships with their unions with these assets in place. This may be contrasted to the antagonistic relationships still found in the United States. A point to remember is that, even companies like Toyota experienced antagonistic labor relationships years ago. After coming

close to bankruptcy and realizing the waste in struggling on the internal matters, management and the unions worked hard to coexist in harmony.

Just as manufacturer-supplier relationships can benefit from the shift from a traditional arms-length relationship to a more enduring friendly relationship with broader perspective as discussed in Chapter 13, union-management relationships may have to change if a company is to remain competitive. Developing mutual trust and a shared understanding of the business is the way to achieve co-destiny.

Chapter 15

Eliminating Problems at the Organizational Boundaries

We have thus far reviewed techniques for improvement in various areas of manufacturing operations and have also touched on people-related issues. With these as a base, we will now turn to organizational issues in the next three chapters.

The goals of our production activities are to manufacture the right product at the right time, in the right quantity, with the highest quality, at the lowest cost, and with the shortest delivery time. Each component of production and production-related activities should fit together to achieve these goals.

TOTAL OPTIMIZATION AND LOCAL OPTIMIZATION

In most cases, people tend to "optimize" their areas of interest without paying enough attention to the broader viewpoint. For example, operators may prefer long production runs with fewer setups if they are focusing on their own operational efficiency. Alternatively, they may work as much as possible to get ahead of schedule in the morning so that they can relax in the afternoon. Similarly, material handlers may like large batches because they require fewer trips for parts

delivery, thus saving time and energy. Or maintenance and inspection people may base their work on their preferences or convenience rather than the priorities determined from the nature of the work. In general, operators who do not have responsibility, or "ownership," of the total process tend not to care about housekeeping, maintenance of their machines, prevention of defects, or production scheduling.

In these examples, operating procedures are developed by people who are specialists in each field. This creates a lack of communication and coordination at the organizational boundaries. People are concerned about how they perform in their own area rather than cooperating with others to achieve the best results for all.

We call this a focus on "local optimization" rather than "total optimization." The model shown in Exhibit 15.1 attempts to convey this point. On the left, three different groups within one organization each focus on their own area of interest. They might represent production activities such as fabrication, subassembly, and final assembly. Or they could be manufacturing, engineering, and marketing; or manufacturers, suppliers, and sales dealerships. We see that each group's narrow focus on its own area results in a lack of communication, a lack of shared goals, and a lack of cooperation.

Exhibit 15.1. A Comparison of Total and Local Optimization

This situation is compared to the organizational model shown on the right of the exhibit where more communication, coordination and cooperation are taking place. The point here is that just-in-time and total-quality-control philosophy, concepts, and techniques can be applied to develop an organization which itself will evolve towards total optimization.

From Local Optimization to Total Optimization

A simple example to describe this point is found in consecutive pro-
duction processes in our factories (see Exhibit 15.2). Operator A pro-
duces products which are processed further by operators B and C.
In between A and B, and B and C, we find inventory that prevents
A, B, and C from communicating, coordinating, and cooperating in
their work. Each operator focuses on his or her own work, but there
is no overall discipline in the pace of work, or consideration of line
balance. Instead, there is a need for supervision, scheduling, trans-
portation of materials, and inspection.

Exhibit 15.2. Operating in an "Isolated Island" Arrangement

This situation is often found not only in fabrication operations
but in assembly operations and other areas as well. Even if each op-
erator is highly skilled, the overall result can be devastatingly inef-
ficient. The term "isolated island" or "a bird in a cage" describes
these situations.

In order to eliminate the waste associated with these situations, several approaches may be developed. For example, quality, cost, and delivery targets may be set that take into account the factors such as the production process, competition, and market trends. These shared targets can motivate every participant in this production arena to work together to achieve these goals.

One solution is to combine three operations to form a "cell," as shown in Exhibit 15.3. With this arrangement, three operators can communicate better, the transportation of materials is reduced, and the inventory between processes is reduced significantly.

Exhibit 15.3. Improvement over "Isolated Island" Arrangement

The Next Process Is Your Customer

As we lower inventory levels and rearrange layouts so that operators can communicate better, we start to visually understand the interrelationships. From operator C's point of view, the next process is shipping. In that sense, the shipping department is C's customer. From operator B's point of view, C is the customer. From operator A's point of view, B is the customer.

Since each operation's goal is simply to comply with the customer's demand, each operator is to work only when his customer demands the product. This is more easily done when individual operations are closer together than when they are arranged in an "isolated island" fashion.

We should realize the importance of producing only what the market requires, especially if that market is volatile and no steady

growth is expected. When this practice is instituted, operators may find themselves idle more often than before. Since they produce only what is required by the customer, operators may also find that there is less confusion as to what items need to be produced and when.

At this stage, the scheduler's role will be reduced. Operators will be able to do routine scheduling by themselves. They can also contribute to improving the quality of the product. This is possible because there is much less inventory and quick feedback of information among operators occurs more than under the previous arrangements. Thus when problems do arise in the new arrangement, the total amount of potential defects is much smaller.

The quick feedback of information to each operator will confirm the notion that the "next process is your customer." Since the customer is nearby and feedback is very fast, any corrective action will be taken much faster. Countermeasures to prevent recurrence of problems will be developed to avoid making the same mistakes again.

When operations are closely linked, the role of the inspector will change. Instead of spending time inspecting and sorting good parts from bad, operators themselves will identify problems and develop countermeasures with the help of quality assurance people. Accordingly, more problem solving and training of operators in such techniques will be done by the inspectors, but less inspection. Operators will start to do the job of quality control by themselves.

The relationship between operators and maintenance people will also change. If buffer inventory is kept low, there is a much greater need to keep machines in good operating condition at all times. Since any machine breakdown can easily stop the entire production, operators will have to be careful to look for any signs of machine failure such as rattles, noise, and overheating. Operators must develop an understanding of oiling procedures, bolt retightening procedures, and other easy maintenance activities. At the first sign of trouble, operators will report it to the maintenance staff. When a problem is found, people will begin to question "why" several times so that the real cause of the problems will be found and corrected.

As in the case of quality control activities, the maintenance people's role changes as operators become capable of doing easy maintenance and problem-solving activities. More preventive maintenance and training of operators will be done and there will be less fire fighting.

As these activities proceed, operators will develop a feeling of

ownership in their operations. They will then guarantee quality, cost, and delivery to the next process.

Flexible Organization

The situation pictured in Exhibits 15.2 and 15.3 in regard to production operations can be applied to other areas as well. Often we find similar weak links at organizational interfaces such as manufacturing and engineering, marketing and manufacturing, and manufacturers and suppliers, to mention a few. (See Exhibit 15.4.) Of course management should coordinate the efforts of these groups with goal congruence in mind, so that instead of win-lose situations favoring one group, win-win situations will be developed.

Exhibit 15.4. Solving Problems at Organizational Boundaries

Exhibit 15.5 illustrates the linkages between manufacturing and design engineering as an example of how two organizations should work together. If these two units cannot communicate easily with each other, the goals of the total organization will suffer.

In order to have these two units work better, many activities have to be coordinated. This may include standardization of parts, designing for manufacturability, engineering changes, and the like. Since the needs of the total organization may change over time, we should be careful not to introduce rigid systems that are difficult to modify.

Exhibit 15.5. Collaboration Between Manufacturing and Design Engineering

This situation is similar to the track relay where slow runners may be helped by faster runners by better utilization of the relay zone. If the zone is very short or not well defined, on the other hand, the coordination between slow and fast runners may be quite limited.

As described previously, the basic principles "simplify, combine, and eliminate" often provide guidelines for improvements. To facilitate this, however, we need management's coordination. As management gives guidance and provides the means for communication, the rest of the activities may be taken care of by the people.

Instead of stifling the organization and suppressing individual abilities, managers should consider each person's ability and promote an environment that allows people to utilize the best of their skills and to help each other.

Management's role, then, is to encourage people to focus more on value-added work so that problem areas are exposed immediately—in effect, to develop the "reflexive muscles" of the organization.

ORGANIZATIONAL STRUCTURE FOLLOWS ECONOMIC NEED

A fundamental notion in business is that "organizational structure should follow economic need." However, if we are not careful, we may emphasize the form or structure more than the substance. We can illustrate this by reviewing the history of industrial engineering (IE) discipline in the United States.

F. W. Taylor's scientific management approach in industrial engineering in the early 1900s has created a group of specialists engaged in IE activities. The unfortunate aspect of this approach is that no

other people are considered capable of practicing IE for operational improvement.

Yet we often find today that most industrial engineers spend little time conducting improvement activities on the shop floor. Instead, they spend most of their time in the office with their papers and files, involved in setting standards for others to follow.

Although there may have been nothing wrong with Mr. Taylor's intent, what was unfortunate was the tendency to allow people whose sole qualifications are advanced academic degrees to monopolize IE techniques. With this monopolized approach, highly trained industrial engineers may be rewarded financially because they have academic degrees, but operators who are actually closest to production activities are neither encouraged to use their practical knowledge to improve work techniques nor financially compensated when they do so. Clearly, this is the case where structure is driving the way people should perform, rather than people following the basic needs of the organization.

In a sellers' market, where products are pushed out into the market with added margin, this may be tolerated. In a buyers' market, however, where competition is keen, products are purchased only as required by customers. In such an environment, the margin is determined by market forces. If an organization does not fit into this competitive environment, then it must adapt to the new environment or it will become extinct.

Example—Mazda

After the oil crisis, Mazda, a Japanese automobile company, was forced to face a tough financial situation. In order to survive, Mazda initiated several programs. From 1977 to 1980, the company dispatched up to 250 of its engineers to suppliers to assist full time with improvement activities and to strengthen the supplier's ties with Mazda. It was called the Bumblebee program since the engineers visited suppliers so frequently, just like bumblebees flying to flowers in order to produce honey.

In the same time period another program, the Model Line program, made managers responsible for improving certain production lines. In fact, until certain levels of improvement were achieved, managers could not leave the shop floor to come back to their offices.

Exhibit 15.6. Mazda's Bumblebee Program

Operators and foremen as well as office workers were also involved in this period. Over time, more than half of the total workforce was sent to car dealers to promote car sales.

As these examples show, manufacturer and suppliers, management and workers, and operators and sales people all worked together in order for Mazda to survive the competition.

Example—Toyota

Toyota is one of the most profitable companies in Japan. Instead of being satisfied with the outstanding performance of its employees, Toyota often reduces the number of people in some of its divisions and reallocates their responsibilities in order to revitalize its organization. After the reduction of head count, the remaining people make a special effort to generate lots of ideas to maintain the same level of production. Of course, the people removed from their previous jobs will assume other responsibilities elsewhere.

In another example, Toyota suddenly closed one affiliated supplier's warehouse and started transporting materials directly from the supplier's factory to Toyota's factory, thereby eliminating unnecessary handling of parts. Naturally, this caused a good deal of confusion at the supplier's plant. With the support of Toyota, however, the supplier's organization was streamlined to follow the new

discipline in a short time. Individuals' responsibilities and the organizational structure were then adjusted to accommodate the change.

Change Is Painful, But Growing Pains Are Necessary

All of the changes we are facing are somewhat painful. But only by expanding our skills and developing flexibility to change can we move forward.

Exhibit 15.7 attempts to convey this point. A number of people are trying to keep the boat afloat. Some are strong, some are weak, some are good at handling buckets, others are good at paddling or handling a rudder. There are lawyers, accountants, salesmen, machine operators, and corporate executives in our manufacturing boat, and all of them are trying to save themselves. There is almost no time to argue about the size of the bucket or paddles or each person's special skills. Everyone simply has to work together to save the boat.

Exhibit 15.7. We Are All in the Same Boat

As shown in this example, organizational boundaries become less of a concern as codestiny is developed among people in maintaining a competitive position and achieving the common goals of the organization. If people focus only on internal disputes, the organization will most likely become extinct. Much depends on an accurate

assessment of current business trends, and wise allocation of the firm's limited resources.

We should not forget that each organization has its own internal opportunities and resources. If everyone involved makes the effort to explore those opportunities and resources with top management's support, progress is indeed possible.

One of the lessons life teaches us is that we *can* develop solutions if we are forced to do so. If we can dream it, we can make it.

SUMMARY

Problems often exist at organizational boundaries. This is because each organization focuses on optimizing its self-interest rather than trying to optimize the total organizational needs. Typical symptoms of this problem are accumulated inventories on the shop floor and piles of paperwork in the office, indicating a lack of communication, coordination, and cooperation.

If we are aware of the amount of waste at the organizational boundaries, however, we should be able to find ways to eliminate it by taking a broader point of view.

The point is simple. We should focus on economic need; organizational structures and systems should follow the need, not the other way around. While change may be painful for those who cling to the past, we should remember that progress comes from challenging the status quo. Like it or not, competition will take care of those who cannot change.

Chapter 16

People Make It Happen

As the problems associated with organizational interfaces are addressed, people will develop a broader perspective about how their own roles fit into the general framework of the organization. As a result, they will be able to contribute more to the organization. In order to realize the importance of people's involvement in our work and to make a smooth transition to better practices, management, staff people, and operators need to review and scrutinize the situation and educate themselves continuously.

CENTRALIZED AND DECENTRALIZED ORGANIZATION

In order to describe the organizational implications of involving people, two types of organizations are compared in Exhibit 16.1. The model on the right indicates that the direct involvement of many people creates a much larger pool of organizational ability than the one on the left where skills and knowledge are centrally controlled.

(Please note that these models are shown here to describe the organization from a vertical viewpoint, whereas the models in Exhibit 15.1 describe the organization from a horizontal viewpoint.)

In the model on the left, skill or knowledge to run a company is concentrated in a small number of management or staff personnel. They issue directions, orders, and schedules for the vast majority of employees. In the factory setting, people's value added may be limited to manual skills in the worst case.

While previous discussions on organizational interfaces indicated

Exhibit 16.1. Comparison of Centralized and Decentralized Organizations

the importance of smooth information flow across the organization, and a broader scope of responsibility for all employees, what we are addressing here is an overburdened management and staff and an underutilized general workforce with only limited contribution potential.

In the model on the right in Exhibit 16.1, on the other hand, large numbers of people are given the opportunity through education and training to contribute their intellectual skills as well as their manual skills. Instead of being directed and monitored, people are in many ways self-controlled, self-thinking, and self-motivated. Management skills are not monopolized by people in the offices.

If we compare the difference of mass in these two models of organization, it should become clear in our eyes which has the competitive advantage in our business world.

Beyond Economies of Scale

The typical argument favoring centralized organization is that of economies of scale. This assumes that smaller, decentralized organizations cannot be as efficient as large centralized ones. In practice, this is rarely the case.

In a centralized organization, a multilevel approval process causes delays in taking appropriate action. Management and staff seem to be governed by their own self-interest, thereby losing touch with their customers. Internal political struggles are common, and stagnation and bureaucracy hinder innovation and improvement efforts.

This situation may be tolerated under a planned economy or a monopolized business, where survival from competitors is not the utmost concern. But in an environment of intense competition, management and staff will be forced to be customer-oriented. They need to work closely with people for survival. Top management should focus on eliminating internal monopolies and encouraging everyone to serve their customers.

One key question is whether or not employees are motivated in their work. The level of employee morale depends on management's leadership. If business competition is based on the development of strategy by top-level management, the involvement of employees may not be a focal point of competitive strength. Accordingly, top management may not pay much attention to "soft" issues such as people' involvement, and employees may be consumed, more or less, like a commodity. As I view the history of U.S. and other Western industries, however, it seems that the overemphasis on the "brain" side of the organization has often resulted in a dichotomy between management and workers (Exhibit 16.2).

Exhibit 16.2. Traditional Structure of Dichotomy

Management		Worker
Boss		Subordinate
Brain	⟵⟶	Muscle
Have		Have not

We are now discovering the limits of a workable corporate strategy development, absent the involvement of people. Even if selected management people develop an innovative strategy, without the support of the rest of the organization that strategy may not be readily executed or the strategic options may be quite narrowed.

Without understanding the human aspects of the organization and the actual operations at the front line, a proposed strategy may not reflect reality, but may be simply an exercise on paper.

The point is rather simple. As in the human body system, the brain itself cannot cause the body to move without the help of other

parts of the body system. Only with a healthy nervous system, bone structure, and musculature can the functions of the brain be carried out.

Extra layers of organization, needlessly long chains of command, and any other wastes in the system should be eliminated in order to maintain a healthy organization. We should never underestimate the capability of people if we want to progress further.

Fear of Losing Control

One major barrier to a smooth transition to the active involvement of all people is management's fear of losing control. When we move from a powerful central authority to a decentralized form, many managers and their staff may feel insecure about their diminishing authority.

Even if we understand the principle that we move ahead by sharing and educating others, it is not necessarily easy to give our accumulated knowledge and experience away. Even though we talk about the involvement of people, we may not practice it well ourselves. We may also fear that sharing our authority and knowledge may make us look foolish if others do not follow suit.

Furthermore, we may argue that (1) others do not have enough knowledge about the company's needs and activities, or (2) they may make mistakes because they lack information or experience, or (3) they may act in their own interest rather than the company's. It was these very fears that led to the development of very hierarchical structures with a powerful centralized authority and resulting rigid organization. The history of mankind gives us millions of examples of people suffering because of these rigid structures. We also find countless examples of rigid hierarchical structures that failed to survive because people spoke up, challenged bureaucracy, freed slaves, demolished old structures and created new ones. Democracy and freedom evolved and equality was sought. Those who clung to the old structures had to give way to a new breed of people who challenged and demolished or reformed the old systems. A point to remember is that we stand now on the foundation created by those who struggled courageously to create a better world.

As we build on that foundation we cannot try to gain control through selfish motives. The rewards from delegating one's responsibilities and involving other people in improvement processes are

the advancement of the organization, and the increased employee motivation. These are the keys to surviving competition. Such efforts will let us advance even into areas we have not been able to address fully before.

Some people may be still concerned about the potential of losing control and creating chaos in the process of delegating responsibility. This is, in a way, a judgmental issue that depends on the quality and motivation of the people involved.

Certainly managers must continue to provide guidance, along with the means to train and educate their employees. They should develop an attitude of letting people try more through delegation of responsibility and practicing tolerance of minor failures if people have done their best.

When we practice this, however, managers are often surprised to find that their people can perform a much greater role than they had expected. The process will take time, and success will depend on the level of commitment by management, managerial style, and the people within the organization.

As we emphasized the need to reduce inventory to make our production system efficient and responsive, we need to reduce the buffer between management and people. Both physical and mental barriers need to be broken down. As Mazda's Bumblebee program reduced the distance between Mazda and its suppliers and their Model Line program enhanced the teamwork between management and operators, a similar approach may be necessary to reduce the distance between management and people.

OWNERSHIP, OWNERSHIP, OWNERSHIP

As we succeed in developing an atmosphere of involvement, we will find much more trust developing within the organization. We will find voluntary relationships rather than the narrowly defined hierarchical relationships.

In this atmosphere of guided autonomy, management's task is to create a supportive environment in which people can have freedom while working toward a common goal. People in the organization will start to speak the same language and share the same philosophy of work.

Management's role will change to one of sponsorship and providing vision for the organization. We should share the notion that

225

these people are the customer from management's point of view. Only through people, is management capable of conducting the business. If you are a manager, can you ask your people the following question: "What can I do to help you to make your job easier?"

Examples

The following examples point out the importance of encouraging the involvement of people.

A few years ago, in the book *In Search of Excellence,* a GM worker, laid off after sixteen years of service in the Pontiac division, was quoted: "I guess I got laid off because I make poor-quality cars. But in sixteen years, not once was I ever asked for a suggestion as to how to do my job better. Not once."

In contrast, a few years ago in a Japanese radio manufacturing factory, a foreign visitor asked an operator, "Isn't it an engineer's job to make such an improvement? Isn't it unnecessary for you to be involved in such an improvement activity?"

The operator's answer was: "I understand what you are saying. But I know this operation better than anyone else in the whole factory. I realized the problem area in my operation and simply made a suggestion to fix it. The idea was accepted and implemented. As a result, the defect rate was reduced significantly. Is there something wrong with this?"

The situation may be changing in western companies. My visits to a number of western factories, however, confirm that the degree of involvement of people is still very low in most cases. Is this because such improvement activity is hard to quantify or to get budget approval for? Is it because no single person can be responsible for and measure his or her own performance?

If we recognize the need for and potential of people involvement, however, can't we do something with the system or structure to accommodate it? If greater involvement is the best solution, shouldn't the system or structure follow that need and enhance people's potential rather than suppress it?

More Examples

In a midwestern manufacturer I have been associated with, a U-shaped layout with two operators (one following the other) was

developed and implemented as part of just-in-time activities (see Exhibit 16.3). This was done on the initiative of manufacturing engineers. The savings were significant, but there were a few problems. The major obstacle was the lack of operator cooperation. For example, the wrong procedure (b) was used by some operators who were somehow convinced that it was more efficient even though the walking distance is much more than the other procedure (a).

Exhibit 16.3. U-Shaped Layout in a U.S. Factory (After Improvement)

a. Right procedure b. Wrong procedure

This company is moving forward with JIT, but in order to facilitate the process, management is starting to focus on developing an understanding of JIT among all employees. Line people are becoming more involved in the activities as information sharing meetings are held and educational videotapes are distributed. Improvement activities are becoming a topic of discussion on the shop floor.

In another California company, similar improvement activities are achieving results. Changing from a functional to a product-oriented layout reduced production lead time from three days to seventeen minutes. A task force approach is used at this company, involving line operators, supervisors, engineers, and maintenance people. The task force met four times before moving ahead with the layout change.

The introduction of the new method was successfully carried out, with colorful balloons celebrating the new line operation. A line su-

Exhibit 16.4. Celebrating a Newly Rearranged Line Operation with Colorful Balloons

pervisor later told me that she had not slept well the night before the changeover because of her excitement and anticipation.

In a Canadian automotive company, some of the industrial engineers were troubled about participating in JIT activities. They could not implement their recommendation for a new setup procedure because of the lack of cooperation from the operators. In other areas of the same factory, however, by simply enhancing communication among different groups of operators involved in a rather complex setup process, the setup time of machines was reduced from an average of twelve hours to six hours within a month.

PEOPLE MAKE IT HAPPEN

There are numerous examples at the factory floor verifying that no system will work unless consideration is given to the people involved. There are also many cases where people made things happen that seemed impossible before.

It is almost a futile battle if the involvement of people is not

given a high priority in the process of improvement activities. If the operators' understanding and involvement are not secured, the improvements simply will not work: Kanban cards may be routinely lost; new work procedures introduced by the engineers may be ignored; better housekeeping will not be practiced, and so on.

When we consider these cases for a moment, it should become obvious to us that these kinds of issues—better housekeeping, product quality, machine breakdowns, number of days on strike, worker morale, number of suggestions, lost kanban cards, compliance to work procedures, level of improvement activities—are all interrelated. Systems make it possible; people make it happen.

Perhaps some people consider this too rudimentary to be taught at business schools or other institutions of higher education, where professional managers emerge with an understanding of advanced concepts, and where "people" issues often take a back seat to measure and analysis. As a result, the dichotomy between management and workers remains. I hope that a bias toward analytical skills will not result in a situation similar to that found in F. W. Taylor's scientific management, where the industrial engineering discipline is monopolized by those who have the "right" academic and paper qualifications.

SUMMARY

Some managers may prefer to remain in their offices, shielded from the factory where the action is taking place. Those are the ones who cannot see the huge potential of people power. Those are the ones who are insecure about abandoning traditional work styles and entering into an unknown and open environment where titles, responsibilities, and office space mean little.

Depending on the commitment level or comfort level with people involvement, the level of progress will differ. Exhibits 16.5 and 16.6 suggest some approaches to be considered.

Most of us are familiar with these approaches. Many may have tried some of them already. The difficulty, however, is putting these approaches into practice by involving everyone to their maximum potential. Any revolutionary change requires a large amount of energy and commitment of people. There is unfortunately no easy solution. But with the understanding of the need for change and with a clear vision of the future, we should be able to make it happen.

Exhibit 16.5 Examples of Approaches to Facilitating People Involvement

- Managing by mingling with operators
- Suggestion program
- Small group improvement activities
- Company newsletter
- Awards (employee of the month, workplace organization award, etc.)
- Quality circle convention
- Posters, banners, and improvement boards
- Sincere concern for each person's problems

Exhibit 16.6. Example of Improvement Posted on the Shop Floor in a Japanese Factory

Chapter 17

Establishing a Competitive Position

In the preface to this book, I mentioned that in terms of individual techniques, there is nothing outstandingly new in this book. Improvement is typically like that. After the fact, it seems so natural when things fit into place. However, what we have addressed here may be compared to the story of the blind men and the elephant.

In the story, the first blind man touches the elephant's trunk (nose), and he thinks that the elephant is a big snake. The second man touches the elephant's ear, thinking it is a thick blanket. Then the third man touches the elephant's leg, thinking it is a tree trunk.

As this story points out, if we are not careful, we may miss the total picture. That is: each set of issues or techniques may be observed and analyzed, yet the total picture or impact is hard to grasp. As a result it is often difficult to implement such techniques and achieve the benefit of their full potential unless we understand how the different pieces fit together.

Furthermore, it is not just the combination of techniques that generates outstanding results. It is the people, with their energy, skills, and shared values, who make things happen. In fact, many of the topics addressed in this book may be considered very low-tech, and full of common sense that many people can practice easily. Because of that, the ideas suggested here may not appeal to those who prefer a more intellectual approach, at least on the surface.

The most powerful results, then, are achieved through the co-

ordination of different techniques and people. In isolation, each may seem insignificant. Nonetheless, the well coordinated efforts of people and techniques often produce unbelievable results. Such is the competitive power of an organization. The basic premise here is that people can perform much more if they are given the right opportunities to utilize their potential skills.

THE FACTORY AS ORCHESTRA

If we compare a factory to a symphony orchestra, we find that a well-performing orchestra has similar characteristics to that of a well-managed factory (see Exhibit 10.1). Each musician has skills that are well developed through extensive training. Each instrument has its own tone and is tuned and well cared for by each player. But there is also a conductor who interprets the music score and coordinates the efforts of all players into a polished performance.

Only when these different elements fit together does the whole orchestra produce an outstanding performance with beautiful harmony, tone, and rhythm. No single element should be missing. No single player or instrument should be out of tune.

In my mind, such is a vision for achieving excellence in manufacturing. All elements should fit together. Each player should understand and conduct his or her role with appropriate consideration to the whole organization. Instead of simply focusing on one area, he or she should be able to share the goals of the whole organization. There should be a score to outline the prescribed performance and a conductor to guide the whole organization to produce to its fullest potential.

As more people understand the vision of the future and the direction of the company, as well as how each individual fits into the picture, the whole system will be effectively integrated and become capable of responding to necessary changes. If this is the case, then, what training is required, and how do the different pieces fit together?

Unfortunately, I do not think that a cookbook-type approach can be recommended for any single organization. Our challenge is to conceive of the broader picture, and to develop the necessary skills to integrate the different pieces of this picture to fit economic needs.

INTEGRATION

Exhibit 17.1 summarizes the characteristics of both a conventional and a progressive company. In the case of the conventional company, the techniques and work orientation of the entire organization have to be challenged as discussed earlier. Otherwise, this company will not be able to compete as a world-class manufacturer.

Exhibit 17.2 also summarizes the key concepts and techniques and their relationships toward eliminating waste as discussed in this book. When these points are addressed and incorporated in the company's operations, the company will have established a superior capability over its competitors in employing its resources. Such is the built-in integrated system we want to establish in place of a collection of piecemeal techniques, systems, equipment, and people.

Exhibit 17.1. Characteristics of Manufacturing in a Conventional and a Progressive Company

	Conventional Company	**Progressive Company**
Operational Characteristic		
Setup time	Long	Short
Lot size	Large	Small
Inventory	Large	Small
Floor space	Large	Small
Transportation	Long	Short
Lead time	Long	Short
Defect rate	High	Low
Machine trouble	High	Low
Organizational Characteristic		
Structure	Rigid	Flexible
Orientation	Local optimization	Total optimization
Communication	Long chain of command	Open communication
Agreement	Contract-based	Trust-based
Union focus	Skill-based	Company-based
Skill base	Narrow	Broad (flexible)
Suppliers	Many	Selected few
Education/training	Insignificant	Significant

Exhibit 17.2. Techniques and Their Relationship Towards Eliminating Waste

The strategy development and execution process should become a much more interactive process among those who are involved. It should be integrated with day-to-day operations as the need to respond quickly to environmental changes increases. Managers and support people can work well with operators and become more effective when they understand each other better. Also, good supplier relationships will be developed by mutual communication and understanding.

Similarly, effective computer integrated manufacturing (CIM) is only possible with a broad understanding of the whole business system. Robots, automated guided vehicles (AGV), computer aided design (CAD), computer aided manufacturing (CAM), computer aided

testing (CAT), computer aided engineering (CAE), flexible manufacturing systems (FMS), and overseas production have to be evaluated under the broad picture as well.

I have seen too many robots, automated warehouses, conveyors, and miscellaneous expensive automated equipment wasted in their application. Some people make the mistake of thinking that advanced manufacturing technology will cure all the problems of manufacturing. It is *not* a cure-all, but it will certainly have applications, especially when such technology can be developed or bought very cheaply and applied wisely.

If technology is developed for the sake of satisfying the specific interest of engineers, however, the application may be unsatisfactory. We need to be very careful about the balance. We need to have the capability to evaluate the different alternatives.

Even though there is a great need for advanced technology, I wonder whether by itself it can support manufacturing industries in today's environment. In my view, there is a lot of room for progress to be gained just by practicing the approaches explained in this book—the so-called low-tech approaches as it may appear.

At least one of the major challenges is for people to work together practicing the fundamentals, collectively. Those companies that seek easy solutions and those that choose the painstaking path will fare differently in the future.

GETTING STARTED

How, then, can we start? Where do we start? Who should we involve? We need to answer these questions before we can move forward. In fact, facing these questions is part of the challenge itself.

Instead of having lengthy discussions in the conference room or immediately seeking an outside expert's help, however, I would recommend starting with at least one project for improvement. Obviously, we do not want this project to fail. We should encourage people and help this project to succeed by providing resources such as people's time, materials, tools, or techniques.

The people involved in this project may vary depending on the nature of the project. A multidisciplinary team approach often helps in dealing with cross-organizational problems. Exhibit 17.3 may serve as a guide to form a project team in various fields.

Exhibit 17.3. Examples of Project and Project Team Members

Level of involvement: 0 = High; • = Medium; Blank space = Low

Area of Focus	Production	Manufacturing Engineer	Quality Assurance	Maintenance	Production Control	Purchasing	Design Engineer
Workplace Organization	0	•	•	•	•		•
Set-up Time Reduction	0	0	•	•	•		
Layout Changes/One Piece Flow Production	0	0	•	•	•		
Low Cost Automation/Simple Dedicated Equipment	0	0	•	•			•
Multifunctional Operators/Job Rotation	0	•	•	•	•		
Jidoka (Line Stop Concept, etc.)	0	0	0	0	•		
Statistical Process Control	0	•	0	•		•	
Poka-Yoke	0	•	0	•		•	•
Visual Control (Andon, etc.)	0	•	0	•	•	•	•
Total Productive Maintenance	0	•	•	0			
Lot Size Reduction	0	•	•		0	•	
Leveled/Mixed Production	0	•	•		0		
Cycle Time Control/Standard Work	0	0	0	•	•		
Kanban, Broadcasting	0	•	•		0	0	
Plant-to-Plant Transportation	•		•	0	•	0	
Supplier Relationships	•	0	0	•	0	0	0
Employee Involvement	0	0	0	0	0	0	0
Parts Commonality	•	•	•				0
Design for Manufacturability	•	•	•			•	0
Value Engineering	0	0	0	•	•	•	0

Note: Manufacturing engineers may include industrial engineers and process engineers.

As we take a look at the Exhibit 17.3, as well as Exhibit 17.2, we will recognize that a lot of linkages among different groups of people, in addition to the linkages among different techniques, have to fit together. Also, as we understand the point of these exhibits, how they are developed, and why, we may want to reconsider the structure of a company's organization in the future so that job responsibility, information linkages, and reporting relationships will not hamper its progress.

In fact, as shown in Exhibit 17.4, much more holistic and per-

Exhibit 17.4. Comparison of Conventional and Biological Organizations

Note: This comparison was developed to illustrate the point on organizational development by Jean Bounine and Kiyoshi Suzaki in *Produire-Juste á Temps* (Paris: Masson, 1986). The concept of biological organization was originally developed by Stafford Beer in *The Brain of the Firm* (London: Allen Lane, 1972).

haps even biological forms of organization may be more suitable for implementing the techniques we have discussed so far and making improvements an ongoing activity. As organization progresses, each person in each organization increases his or her skills and becomes a vital part of the whole.

Such is the vision of the future company organization in my mind. But before we can get things moving and pick up momentum, there are still many obstacles to be removed. What we can do, though, is move forward a step at a time. Then the organizational structure can simply follow.

Since one of our objectives is for people to gain confidence and internalize the process of improvement, they should not necessarily be directed. They are the customers to whom we want to sell our ideas. We want everyone to develop a sense of ownership. Our vision is to develop a self-controlled, self-thinking, and self-motivated organization.

We also want improvement activities to become a way of life (remember that there is no end to improvement). Therefore, we want to make improvement a habit. If we take this position, we should be able to start our improvement activities every day from ground zero.

In selecting the initial project, however, we want to choose one with a high probability of achieving success over a relatively short time period so that confidence will develop quickly. Also, we want this project to be highly visible to others since we want to share the success by boosting people's morale as much as possible.

When success is achieved, we should provide quick feedback to those who contributed to it, and publicize this success to others in the organization. This will help to create an atmosphere conducive to further improvement.

Specifically, we can use display boards in the factory, employee newsletters, videotapes, meetings, and so on. We may have people visiting and exchanging ideas in the project area. We may have people talking about the successful project in various corners of the factory. Clearly, if the project eliminates positions, we need to address the issue of job security. In a nutshell, the process of improvement follows the cycle shown in Exhibit 17.5.

First, people must be provided with the necessary tools and directions. These may take the form of books, videos, training manuals, exchange visits, on-the-job training, and the like. Through this

Exhibit 17.5. Cycle of Improvement

training and educational process, people will learn basic improvement techniques. Other kinds of tools may be provided through small group improvement activities, quality circles, or suggestion programs where people can apply available techniques to their own creativity.

Second, management must provide a supportive environment that encourages employees to use the tools in the most appropriate way. This is where consideration for the people involved is needed most. Without this, even the most well-designed program will not work—especially when such a program requires participation from many people from different disciplines.

Developing trust between management and employees is important. Management's closeness to employees and their visibility on the factory floor should provide room to do things together. Positive reinforcement, rather than a rigidly followed chain of command, means a lot in developing favorable value systems in the factory.

Third, when the tools are provided and the use of tools is encouraged, the results need to be shared by everyone involved. This feedback process should be quick and visible to everyone.

Once through this cycle, we can provide more tools for people to practice or expand improvement activities to other areas. By going through these three major steps a number of times, we can develop a culture that makes improvement a way of life.

GUIDED AUTONOMY

We have now covered issues related to people and techniques. We have also examined approaches to establishing a company's competitive position. Management's role should, then, become clear from understanding the needs of the organization, as well as the need to implement the techniques, concepts, and philosophy we have discussed thus far.

The first step in achieving this understanding, however, is to make a commitment to the project at hand. We need to select people and an area of focus, allocate resources, and be fully committed to

Exhibit 17.6. Summary of JIT/TQC Activities for Five U.S. Companies

COMPANY NAME (DIVISION)	PRODUCT CATEGORY	PRODUCTION CHARACTERISTICS	START/ REPORTING PERIOD	WHO INITIATED ACTION?	WHY STARTED?	WHERE STARTED?	HOW IMPLEMENTED	PROBLEMS OBSERVED
Deere & Company	• Hvy. machinery • Farm equip. • Lawn-care equip.	• Repetitive manufacturing	• 1980 • 1982-1984	• CEO/mfg. managers (trip to Japan) • Steering committee	• Survival • Foreign competition	• Four plants	• Visit to Japan • Task force in plant • Education • Pilot projects • Work-flow analysis	• Initially, worker doubts • Underestimated educational needs
Black & Decker (Consumer power tools)	• Electrical products	• Repetitive manufacturing • Floor space 385,000 ft² • Employees: 1,010	• 1982 • 1982-1984	• Staff • Prod'n control committee	• Large expenses in inventory carrying costs (high interest rate)	• Assembly • Purchasing	• Education • Balanced flow • Rewrote work procedures • Started to produce in weekly qty.	• Vendor resistance • Resistance to change
Omark Industries	• Forestry equip. and sporting goods	• Mostly repetitive • 18 plants	• 1980/ Jan. • 1981-1983	• CEO (trip to Japan) • Corporate task force • Plant study teams	• Corporate task force found JIT/TQC/ employee involvement as reason for success	• Five pilot plants	• Steering committee • Plant study team • Presentation by corporate staff • Pilot projects	• Middle mgmt. resistance • Underestimated training needs • Slowdown after first projects
Hewlett-Packard (Computer Systems Division)	• Computer & test systems	• Forming/ Assembly/ Testing • Many options	• TQC: 3 years • JIT: 1 year (1983-1984)	• Steering committee	• Questioned why overseas suppliers produced quality products	• Ass'y flow rearrangement	• TQC first • Employee training/ involvement • Leveled schedule • Process simplification	• Cut WIP levels too quickly • Major changes faster than could assimilate
FMC	• Indus'l equip. • Defense • Automotive • Electrical	• Multiple divisions with variety of products • 50 mfg. and mining operations	• 1982 • 1982-1984	• Operation's support staff • VP-Mfg. • Controller	• Survival • Absence of patent protection • Keen cost competition	• Pilot projects • Automotive and electrical: well-managed op'n first	• Seminars • Pilot Proj. • Pilot plants • Setup time • Inventory target • Positive reinforcement	• Fine-tuning • Not enough manpower to implement ideas • Occasional line stop from parts shortage

From Kiyoshi Suzaki, "Comparative Study of JIT/TQC Activities in Japanese and Western Companies," First World Congress of Production and Inventory Control, Vienna, Austria, 1985, pp. 63–66.

making progress. Furthermore, management needs to help create a supportive environment, monitor progress, share results, and provide support to people.

The last point of this managerial process is especially different from conventional practices, and unfortunately is often ignored by many in spite of its importance. For today's managers, however, the ability to guide and support people becomes a key for improvement.

Perhaps a better term than "management" to convey this notion is "leadership." By providing a vision of the future, and guiding people to develop pride and ownership in their work, a leader-manager can create an energy in the organization which no one using the traditional style of management can accomplish.

Exhibit 17.6. (*Continued*)

COMPANY NAME (DIVISION)	START/ REPORTING PERIOD	LABOR PRODUCTIVITY IMPROVEMENT	SETUP TIME IMPROVEMENT	INVENTORY REDUCTIONS	QUALITY IMPROVE-MENTS	SPACE SAVINGS	PRODUCTION LEAD TIMES	EFFECT ON CORPORATE CULTURE	COMMENTS
Deere & Company	• 1980 • 1982-1984	• Subassembly: 19%-35% • Welding 7%-38% • Mfg. cost: 10%-20% • Material handling 40%	• Presses: 38%-80% • Drills: 24%-33% • Shears: 45% • Grinders: 44% • Avg. 45%	• Raw steel: 40% • Purchased parts 7% • Crane shafts: 30 days-3 days ➤ • Avg: 31%	• Imple-mented process control charting in 40% of opera-tions	• Signif-icant	• Signif-icant	• Unexpec-ted en-thusiam • More re-sponsive to all • Increased employee partic'n	• Japan's Yanmar Diesel's support • Did not introduce TQC in the be-ginning
Black & Decker (Consumer power tools)	• 1982- • 1982-1984	• Assembly: 24 operators→ 6 operators • Support: 7 ➤ 5	• Punch press: 1 hr.→ 1 min. • Drastic in many areas	• Turns: 16→30	• Reduced com-plaints in pack-aging 98% • 100& cus-tomer service level	• Signif-icant	• Products made in weekly lots 50% ➤ 95%		• Number of suppliers reduced by 40% • Quality audit of suppliers
Omark Industries	• 1981/ Jan. • 1981-1983	• Plant A: 30% • Plant B: 30% • Plant C: 20%	• A: 165➤ 5 min. • B: 43→ 17 min. • C: 360→ 17 min. • D: 45➤ 6 min.	• Product A: 92% • Product B: 29% • Product C: 50%	• Product A scrap & rework: 20% • Product E Customer service cost: 50%	• Parts travel distance: Product C: 24% Product E: 68%	• A: 3 weeks ➤ 3 days • E: 21 days → 3 days	• Hourly workers making decisions • High employee involve-ment	• JIT/TQC at the same time
Hewlett-Packard (Computer Systems Division)	• TQC: 3 yrs. • JIT: 1 yr. (1983-1984)	• Standard hours: 87 hrs. ➤ 39 hrs.	Not available	• PC Ass'y inventory $675,000 (100) ➤ $190,000 (28)	• Solder defects: 5000 PPM ➤ 100 • Scrap: $80,000/ mo. ➤ $5,000	• PC Ass'y: 8,500 ft.2 ➤ 5,750 ft.2	• PC Ass'y 15 days→ 1.5 days	• Corporate culture (H-P way) helped JIT • Proud to be among first to implement JIT/TQC	• Adopted TQC/JIT separ ately • MRP did not support JIT
FMC	• 1982 • 1982-1984	• Direct labor prod'y: 13% (Automotive service equipment division)	• Defense equipment group: 60%-75% • Automo-tive/ electri-cal: 80%	• Turns: 1.9 ➤ 4.0 (Automo-tive service equipment division)	• Customer service: 88% ➤ 98% • Cost of quality: 3.5% ➤ 2.1% (Auto.Svc. Eq. Div.)	• Auto-motive/ electri-cal: 25% • Elimi-nated stockroom	• Auto-motive/ electri-cal: 1 mo. -➤ 1 wk • Suppliers: months ➤ days	• Grass-roots movement toward mfg. ex-cellence	• Reduced suppliers by 50% • Corporate plan to implement TQC/JIT at all plants by 1986

Developing a Frame of Reference

In order for us to develop a vision of the future, it is often beneficial to develop a frame of reference in our minds. To do this, more than thirty western and Japanese companies were studied in their approaches to and degrees of accomplishment in JIT/TQC activities. From these companies, ten are compared in Exhibits 17.6 and 17.7.

As seen from the exhibits, there are many differences in product and production characteristics, length of JIT/TQC implementation, level of achievement, and so on, as well as differences in intangible characteristics such as management philosophy, culture, worker mo-

Exhibit 17.7. Summary of JIT/TQC Activities for Five Japanese Companies

COMPANY NAME (DIVISION)	PRODUCT CATEGORY	PRODUCTION CHARACTERISTICS	START/ REPORTING PERIOD	WHO INITIATED ACTION?	WHY STARTED?	WHERE STARTED?	HOW IMPLEMENTED	PROBLEMS OBSERVED
Canon	• Camera • Office equip., etc.	• Repetitive • Employees: 31,000	• 1973 • 1976-1983	• Top management	• Survival • Oil crisis • Failure in hand calculators business (1974)	• Education of waste elimination at all plants • QA • Flow production	• Visual control • Awareness development • Stick with plans • Upgrading speedup	• Misc. problems were observed but solved by enhanced capability of people
Hitachi	• Home appl. • IC • Computer • Ind'l, transportation eq., etc.	• Various 35 factories • Employees: 80,000 • Products: 20,000 kinds	• N.A. • 1977-1981	• Plant top mgmt. • Coordination with corporate	• Intense competition	• Evolutionary • Plant independent	• Education • Plant independent • Later, coordination among plants	• Needed to develop managerial indices to keep track of different plant performances
Yanmar	• Diesel engines • Tractors	• Repetitive • Employees: 6,000	• 1974 • 1975-1981	• Relationship of top mgmt. with Toyota	• Oil crisis • Cost increase • More variety of products	• Education • Elimination of waste	• 'Step by step' • Education • Housekeeping • Elimination of waste	• Extensive needs for education
Mazda	• Automobiles	• Repetitive • Employees: 30,000	• 1973 • 1973-1981	• Top management • Bank executives	• Oil crisis Survival • Evolutionary	• Evolutionary	• Set goals to cut WIP 50% every year • Three pilot lines per factory • Supplier program	• Supplier capability • People's motivation plays an essential part in changes • Needed to share common objectives
Tokai Rika	• Automotive parts	• Repetitive • Employees: 4,100	• 1973 • 1973-1982	• Top management • Promoters in each shop	• Oil crisis • Slower growth • More variety	• Trial introduction in one plant • Expansion	• Study (6 mo) • Trial (6 mo) • Expansion & tune-up (1975-) • Checkup by Toyota • Corporate support	• Intermittent plant disorders • Supported by top management, however

From Kiyoshi Suzaki, "Comparative Study of JIT/TQC Activities in Japanese and Western Companies," First World Congress of Production and Inventory Control, Vienna, Austria, 1985, pp. 67–68.

rale, and labor relationships. However, many common characteristics are derived from the study. Major findings are summarized in Exhibit 17.8.

A point to remember here is that the level of improvement and corresponding period for the improvement are merely indices. What is more important to recognize is that there is no end to improvement. For example, Toyota is striving to achieve a 10 percent or more annual improvement in labor productivity even after many years of significant accomplishment. As this example indicates, developing a sustainable competitive advantage requires continuous efforts in fully utilizing the company's resources.

While these references may be helpful in stimulating our imag-

Exhibit 17.7. (*Continued*)

COMPANY NAME (DIVISION)	START/ REPORTING PERIOD	LABOR PRODUCTIVITY IMPROVEMENT	SETUP TIME IMPROVEMENT	INVENTORY REDUCTIONS	QUALITY IMPROVE-MENTS	SPACE SAVINGS	PRODUCTION LEAD TIMES	EFFECT ON CORPORATE CULTURE	COMMENTS
Canon	• 1973 • 1976-1983	• (Indexed) 100 → 250 • Savings through elim. of waste: $15M ('76) → $90M('82)	• Accessory parts op'n: 4 min. → 15 sec.	• (Indexed) 100 ('76) → 50 ('82)	• 45% reduction of defects in 3 mo. (parts machining factory)	• Factor of three (copier assembly line)	• Signif-icant	• Revital-ized work force • Respect for indi-vidual & workplace	• Good match at system & people
Hitachi	• N.A. • 1977-1981	• (Indexed) 100 → 178	• Sheet metal line: 160 min. → 5 • Machining center: 245 min → 9 min. • 250-ton die cast: 75 min→3	• (Indexed) 100 ('77) → 60 ('81) (S. fac-tory re-frig. line)	• Signif-icant	• Signif-icant	• 20 days→3 days (S fac-tory)	• Many sug-gestions from em-ployees: (30 sug-gestions/ employee month: S factory)	• Use of kanban, warning lamp, & lane system
Yanmar	• 1974 • 1975-1981	• (Indexed) 100 → 191	• Alum. die cast: 125→ 6 min. • Cyl. block machining line: 633 min. →10	• (Indexed) 100 ('75) → 35 ('80) • 81 days ('75) → 29 days ('80)	• Product A Defects: 100 → 56 • Product B Defects: 100 → 18	• Signif-icant	• Signif-icant	• Emphasis on inquis-itive mind and chal-lenging spirit	
Mazda	• 1973 • 1973-1981	• (Indexed) 100 → 215 • 70%-80% of gain from elim. of waste	• Ring gear cutter: 390 min. → 13 min. ('80)	• (Indexed) 100 ('73) → 31 ('81)	• Signif-icant • Machine down time reduced 50-60 hours/ month	• Signif-icant	• Signif-icant	• # of sug-gestions: 2.2 mil. (1981) • Savings from emp. sugg'ns: $11 mil. in 1979	• Reduction of direct workers by 10,000 in 8 yrs. while produc-tion doubled
Tokai Rika	• 1973 • 1973-1982	• (Indexed) 100 → 145 • Equivalent to 317 people	• Die cast: 40 min. → 2 min. 90 min. → 20 sec.	• (indexed) 100 ('75) → 35 ('76)	• Signif-icant	• Signif-icant • Elimin-ation of ware-houses • Many U-lines	• Signif-icant	• Smooth human re-lationship • Increased motivation • Strong top mgmt. direction	• Hard work is nec'y • Toyota's support • Self-made machines • Do-it-yourself spirit

Exhibit 17.8. Major Findings of JIT/TQC Activities from Japanese and Western Companies

Benefits observed from JIT/ TQC:	Significant, both for repetitive and job shop
Motivating forces for implementation:	Survival; pressure from outside; understanding of concepts
Approaches for implementation:	Total company activity; employee involvement
Implementation process:	Incremental, rather than step functional improvements; a journey rather than a trip
Education:	Need for conceptual as well as technical understanding
Organizational issues:	Job security; orientation toward total optimization; self-controlled, self-motivated organization

From Kiyoshi Suzaki, "Comparative Study of JIT/TQC Activities in Japanese and Western Companies," First World Congress of Production and Inventory Control, Vienna, Austria, 1985, p. 68.

ination for improvement, actual visits to the companies and meeting people with experience are also advised, especially for those with limited experience. Seeing people practicing innovative techniques with our own eyes and getting ideas directly from them may give us more information than hours spent in seminars.

The point is that we can improve our operations as much as we can imagine. If, instead, we think we have already accomplished a great deal, there will be a limit to our progress. Similarly, those who spend time looking for excuses may have a hard time making improvements. We just have to be positive, and constructive.

If Toyota had listened to the operators who said that the setup time for a 1000-ton press could not be reduced from a few hours, they wouldn't have achieved the three-minute setup operations they accomplished by 1971. Similarly, if we listen to assembly operators who complain that mixed production makes their work more difficult, we will never achieve the numerous benefits associated with it. If we are limited by job classifications, we may be tied to a rigid structure for years to come (if we are lucky to survive at all). If people are accustomed to doing manual work sitting on chairs, they may resist the change to a standing position—even if it ultimately proves less tiring and healthier to do so.

Constrained by the preconceived notions found in these cases,

we may not be able to imagine the potential benefit of new ideas. Instead, we may be limiting our progress. We may grasp an idea intellectually, but our hearts may not be in it enough to put it into practice. It is for this reason that I would like to stress the following seven points:

1. *Challenging conventional beliefs*—without challenge, there will be no progress.
2. *Bias toward experimentation*—by actually trying new ideas, various problems become known.
3. *Tolerance for failure*—improvement requires patience.
4. *Trust*—improvement will not be tied to layoffs.
5. *Teamwork*—total optimization rather than local (individual) optimization.
6. *Flexibility*—rigid structures will limit progress.
7. *Discipline*—stick to standards.

Continuous Improvement

When some level of achievement has been attained after the initial challenge, people tend to relax. They may start to ask "Isn't this good enough?" But as we have pointed out again and again, there is no end to improvement. What we have been discussing here cannot be compared to a day's hike or a weekend trip. Rather, it is a lifelong journey.

In fact, as we progress, the focus of our efforts may expand to other areas of the business. From design-manufacturing cooperations such as design for manufacturability or quick production start-up for a new product to sales-manufacturing cooperations such as reduction of information lead time from order taking to shipping, we should be able to expand our efforts in streamlining business operations.

A point to recognize is that we should not be simply applying a technique such as reducing setup times or producing "flow" on the shop floor for its own sake. Just-in-time (JIT), total quality control (TQC), total productive maintenance (TPM), computer integrated manufacturing (CIM) and the like, are merely tools to achieve goals.

Yet in many cases these may be considered as goals themselves. It is for this reason that top management should play a major role in providing leadership and guiding the people in the organization.

By constantly asking "What should the company be doing?" we should build new systems and then destroy them to rebuild improved systems. This is the process of continual effort for improvement.

If we introduce certain techniques or concepts just because others are doing so, how can a company build up a competitive advantage? We simply have to go beyond this in our challenge to differentiate us from competitors. For example, TQC would not have been born in Japan if the Japanese people had simply imported the concept of quality control from the United States without adapting it to fit their situation. Instead, the original concept was expanded to significantly involve first line operators and to address the quality of management as well as the quality of product as initially aimed for.

Just-in-time philosophy is also expanding from a production system to a management system. TPM and CIM are following the same course in our pursuit for progress.

In today's competitive business world, a message from one of our predecessors still holds true: "Even if we are on the right track, we will get run over if we just sit there." In this sense, each person, each organization constantly needs to seek ways for continuous improvement.

What Is Manufacturing Strategy?

We use and hear buzz words such as "corporate strategy" or "manufacturing strategy" in our business life. If we are not careful, however, these words themselves may be viewed as a trace of Taylorism. We may think that those who develop the strategy, and direction have authority to do so without involving the people. Is this really and truly effective in today's environment?

By using certain assumptions and gathering comparative data, resources can be allocated to better position the company. There is nothing wrong with this process. But are these assumptions always appropriate? Where is the room for people to contribute or challenge their potential abilities? Aren't those who do the analysis similar to the industrial engineers in the traditional sense, who sit in their offices away from the shop floor?

In contrast to this orientation, when I visited one of Toyota's affiliates in 1985, I heard one of Toyota's top managers comment to the management of this affiliate that the position of the palm button switch in one operation was too high above the shoulder level of the

operator. The impact on the surrounding people was significant. The question remains: "How strategically important is it to take such an action?"

In my mind this small incident seems to raise an important question about the way strategy is typically developed and executed in Western industries. Let us therefore ask ourselves: "What are our roles in developing competitive positions for the company?" "How can we contribute to achieving a competitive position?"

From what we have studied thus far, we should be able to respond to these questions at least in the following manner: One of our important goals is to increase the value-added portion of activities in our worklife by thinking of ways to do this, by practicing these ideas, and by conveying these messages to all company employees. To me, such an orientation has a very important strategic value to companies today.

THE NEW MANUFACTURING CHALLENGE

The challenge for today's manufacturers is great. I see many people working hard to regain a competitive edge in manufacturing. Yet there is no question that fierce competition will take its toll on some manufacturing companies, if not many.

There will be a lot of questions asked of management about the approaches and decisions related to manufacturing activities. Managers are required to develop a coherent and integrated vision to answer those questions.

I certainly hope this book has given readers something to think about and to use. I believe each specific technique is important. People issues are a key. I do not think the abilities of people are different around the world. It is a matter of how to coordinate people and techniques to create a competitive position.

In 500 B.C., Sun Tzu commented in his book *The Art of War* as follows: "All men can see the tactics whereby I conquer, but what none can see is the strategy out of which victory is evolved." To this end, I wish everyone the best in his or her own endeavors.

Epilogue: Vision
of the Future

In order to complete this book, I freed myself from my work for several months. Rescrutinizing the manuscript, its logic, content, and the use of examples away from home, I realized that it was still far from completion. Unfortunate as it may be, I am also aware that there is no end to improvement. In that sense, a book of this kind is a testament to that notion.

I did not want this book to be considered a cookbook, even though there may be elements of that. Rather, I wanted it to portray a vision of the future and provide certain guidelines to move us forward. I wanted to touch on techniques that are developed as a result of human ingenuity instead of proposing "*the* techniques" as cure-alls. I also wanted to tie techniques to people and organizational issues in order to convey the notion of "user-friendly" system.

Because of these concerns, I did not especially emphasize imposing a rigid framework or specific logic in the book. Instead, I intended the use of numerous illustrations and exhibits to convey my message in a gentler fashion.

In this regard, this book addresses the importance of the right side of the human brain where visionary or intuitive thinking takes place in addition to the left side, where logic is formulated and processed.

Improvements are like inventions. If we are motivated, and persistent enough to believe that we can accomplish something, then we will realize our dreams. History has proven this over and over. It is

a challenge to the established structures, assumptions, old systems, and habits that I wanted to convey from this book. It is an imagination for the future and an optimistic thinking which will keep us moving forward.

While I have focused on the subject of manufacturing in this book, many of the concepts discussed here are relevant to other areas of business. Anything that prevents us from achieving maximum quality, minimum price, and prompt delivery to our customers constitutes waste.

In 1922 Henry Ford said, "Thinking always ahead, thinking always of trying to do more, brings a state of mind in which nothing is impossible. The moment one gets into the 'expert' state of mind a great number of things become impossible."

In the 1970s Taiichi Ohno said, "By actually trying, various problems became known. . . . As such problems became gradually clear, they taught me the direction of the next move."

It is the humbleness and challenging spirit of both these men that I respect. We must never stop questioning, never stop challenging, and we must develop an attitude for betterment and act upon it.

Bibliography

Bounine, J. and Suzaki, K. *Produire Juste a Temps—Les Sources de la Productivité Industrielle Japonaise.*: Masson, 1986

Deming, W. E. *Out of the Crisis.* Cambridge, Mass.: Massachusetts Institute of Technology, 1986.

Ford, H. *My Life and Work.* London: Heinemann, 1922.

——. *Today and Tomorrow.* Garden City, NY: Garden City Publishing Company., 1926.

——. *Moving Forward.* Garden City, NY: Doubleday, Doran & Co., 1930.

Fukuda, R. *Managerial Engineering.* Stamford, Connecticut: Productivity, Inc., 1983.

Hall, R. *Zero Inventories.* Homewood Ill: Dow Jones Irwin, 1983.

Hayes, R. and Wheelwright, S. *Restoring Our Competitive Edge: Competing Through Manufacturing.* New York: John Wiley, 1984.

Imai, M. *Kaizen.* New York: Random House, 1986.

Ishikawa, K. *What Is Total Quality Control? Japanese Way.* Englewood Cliffs, NJ: Prentice-Hall, 1985.

Japan Management Association. *Kanban—Just In Time at Toyota.* : Productivity Press, 1986.

Monden, Y. *Toyota Production System.* Atlanta: Institute of Industrial Engineers, 1983.

Peters, T. and Austin, N. *A Passion for Excellence.* New York: Random House, 1985.

Peters, T. and Waterman, R. *In Search of Excellence.* New York: Harper & Row, 1982.

Pinchot, G. *Intrapreneuring.* New York: Harper & Row, 1985.

Schonberger, R. *Japanese Manufacturing Techniques.* New York: The Free Press, 1982.

——. *World Class Manufacturing*. New York: The Free Press, 1986.

Shingo, S. *Study of Toyota Production System from Industrial Engineering Viewpoint*. Tokyo: Japan Management Association, 1981.

——. *A Revolution in Manufacturing: The SMED System*. Stamford Connecticut: Productivity, Inc., 1985.

——. *Zero Quality Control: Source Inspection and the Poka-yoke System*. Stamford, Conn.: Productivity, Inc. 1986.

Skinner, W. *Manufacturing: The Formidable Competitive Weapon*. New York: John Wiley, 1985.

Suzaki, K. Corporate Culture for JIT. APICS Zero Inventory Philosophy and Practice Seminar, St. Louis, 1984.

——. "Work-in-Process Management: An Illustrated Guide to Productivity Improvement." *Production and Inventory Management,* Fall 1985.

——. Application of JIT Concept at Fireplace Manufacturers, Inc. APICS fall seminar, Las Vegas, 1985.

——. Comparative Study of JIT/TQC Activities in Japanese and Western Companies. First World Congress of Production and Inventory Control, Vienna, 1985.

——. Japanese Manufacturing Practices and Their Diffusion in U.S. Industries. Liaisons Sociales' Conference on Prospects of Employment in Industrial Societies, Paris, October 1985.

——. "Japanese Manufacturing Techniques: Their Importance to U.S. Manufacturers." *Journal of Business Strategy,* Winter 1985.

——. JIT and Worker Participation. APICS Annual Conference, Toronto, 1985.

——. Establishing the Competitive Position with Just-in-Time, Just-in-Time Conference by Gesellschaft für Management and Technologie mbH, Böblingen, October 1986.

JAPANESE PUBLICATIONS

Nakajima, S. et al. *TPM Evolution Program*. Tokyo: Japan Institute of Plant Maintenance, 1982.

Ohno, T. *Toyota Production System*. Tokyo: Diamond Publishing Company, 1978.

——. *Taiichi Ohno's Work Site Management*. Tokyo: Japan Management Association, 1982.

Suzaki, K. *Just-in-Time Revolution*. Tokyo: Diamond Publishing Company, 1987.

Suzaki, K. et al. "The New Wave of Toyota Production System." *Factory Management,* May 1985.

Index